MAKE YOUR OWN
ALTERNATIVE ENERGY

MAKE YOUR OWN
ALTERNATIVE
ENERGY

Richard Cummings

DAVID McKAY COMPANY, INC.
New York

To the kids of New Hope Farm (jacket photo):
Marc Arnold, 11, Helge Arnold, 15, Payge, 17,
Allie Votta, 13, Debbie Corbett, 17, Brian
Mlodzinski, 8, Jessie Mlodzinski, 4, Lisa
Kaartinen, 17, and Johnny Abraham, 70.

Library of Congress Cataloging in Publication Data

Gardner, Richard M
  Make your own alternative energy.

  Bibliography: p.
  Includes index.
  SUMMARY: Describes solar, water, and wind
power, nuclear energy, and integrated systems and
their role in the future. Includes instructions
for making projects and experiments.
  1. Renewable energy sources—Juvenile literature.
[1. Renewable energy sources. 2. Power resources]
I. Title.
TJ163.23.G37   621.4   78-20316
ISBN 0-679-20804-6

1 2 3 4 5 6 7 8 9 10

Manufactured in the United States of America

CONTENTS

INTRODUCTION   1

1   ALTERNATIVE ENERGY   3

2   SOLAR POWER   11

How to Make an Instant Solar Collector. How to Build
a Passive-System Solar Greenhouse. How to Make an
Instant Solar Water Heater. How to Build a Thermosiphoning Solar Water Heater. How to Make a Reflecting
Solar Cooker. How to Make a Solar Still.

3   WATER POWER   63

How to Make a Hydraulic Marble Machine. How to
Build a Waterwheel Rock Tumbler. How to Make
an Experimental Pelton Wheel.

4   WIND POWER   87

How to Make a Calibrated Wind Gauge. How to Build
a Bicycle-Wheel Wind Plant. How to Make a Savonius
Rotor Fish-Pond Agitator.

5   NUCLEAR ENERGY   113

6 OTHER ALTERNATIVES   119

How to Make Fireplace Logs from Newspapers. How to Build a Sawdust Stove. How to Make a Tabletop Methane Digester.

7 INTEGRATED SYSTEMS   139

How to Develop an Integrated Aquaculture System.

METRIC CONVERSION TABLE   **146**
APPENDIX   **147**
   BOOKS   **147**
   MAGAZINES   **149**
   SUPPLIERS   **150**
INDEX   **152**

INTRODUCTION

This book is a short manual on alternatives to today's energy systems. It includes plans for experiments and for building alternative energy machines and models. It is divided into seven chapters, each chapter representing an energy category: (1) Alternative Energy (in general); (2) Solar Power; (3) Water Power; (4) Wind Power; (5) Nuclear Energy; (6) Other Alternatives; (7) Integrated Systems.

There are two keys to the information in this book. If you are interested in a general energy category, see the Contents on page v. The experiments and models are also listed there.

If you are curious about a particular energy term, problem, or device, consult the alphabetical Index at the back of the book. Suppliers of equipment and materials are listed in the Appendix.

OIL DERRICKS
SPINDLETOP, BEAUMONT,
TEXAS — 1902 —

1
ALTERNATIVE ENERGY

What Is Alternative Energy?

The term *alternative energy* came into popular use following the Arab oil embargo of 1973. In that year, the oil-producing nations of the Middle East briefly stopped providing oil to the major industrial nations, particularly the United States, Great Britain, Germany, France, and Japan. Once the oil producers had given their major customers a good scare, they sharply raised the price of oil, and have raised it several times since then. People and institutions in the affected countries began to worry that they might run out of the fuel needed to power their great industrial plants, heat their homes, and run their cars and trucks. They began to seek alternative sources of power and energy to what are called the fossil fuels: petroleum, coal, and natural gas.

    Alternative: a necessary or remaining course or choice.

    Energy: available power; the capacity to do work.

In this book, *alternative energy* is defined as any possible source of energy other than that resulting directly from the consumption of fossil fuels. This includes solar, wind, water, wood, and others. Nuclear energy is a special case. Although it is extracted from a fossil fuel (uranium), it is considered by some to

3

be the best alternative to the use of the traditional fossil fuels. However, because of nuclear energy's less promising characteristics, we have concentrated on nuclear power in Chapter Five.

Where Does Our Present Energy Come From?

Figure 4, *A*, shows the main sources of energy used in the United States. Over 40 percent comes from the consumption of petroleum products, nearly half of which are imported from other countries. Thirty-four percent comes from natural gas; 20 percent from coal. Our hydroelectric dams and turbine engines produce only 4 percent of our energy, and nuclear reactors presently supply a minuscule 1.5 percent of U.S. energy needs.

Section *B* of Figure 4 shows where that energy goes. Twenty-five percent is used for the production of electricity, both for industry and for private home use. Almost half of all the energy produced is lost during transmission from one place to another—lost through mechanical inefficiencies and incomplete burning. About 20 percent is used by industry. Twenty-five percent is used to fuel our 93 million cars and 185,000 planes, plus ships, boats, trucks, buses, tractors, and other vehicles. Another 25 percent goes to residential and commercial lighting, cooking, air conditioning, and electrical appliances. Thirty percent of the energy resulting from the burning of fossil fuels is used in the process of mining and refining additional fuel.

This costly and wasteful dependence on fossil fuels reached a peak by 1970. It also became increasingly apparent that fossil fuels produce unpleasant side effects, such as industrial illnesses and water and air pollution. Then, in 1973 came the shock of the Arab oil embargo.

Didn't Anybody Guess What Was Coming?

Yes. An eventual shortage of fossil fuels has been predicted by geologists for many decades. As always, far-sighted scientists, engineers, and inventors had begun seeking alternatives. For instance, about 100 years ago a French naturalist built a large solar furnace that ran a steam engine (see Figure 5).

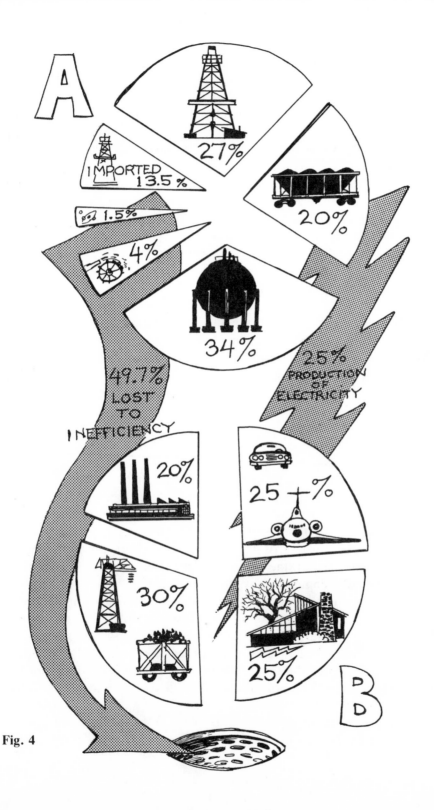

Fig. 4

Are the Fossil Fuels Really Almost Gone?

Opinions vary. There is probably enough information available right now to predict exactly when we will run out of each of the fossil fuels, but the answers are being confused by debates and competition between various political and economic forces. Some experts say that the world will run out of petroleum and natural gas in exactly 31 years; others claim there is enough for the next 200 years. Most experts agree that there is enough coal for many hundreds, even thousands, of years, but they disagree on the practicality of digging it up.

Is the Supply Limited?

Definitely. And it is virtually nonrenewable. Once it is gone, it is gone forever. Each ton of coal, barrel of oil, and cubic foot of natural gas took hundreds of thousands of years to form in the earth's crust (see Figure 6). In a single year, we use up 6 billion tons of these carbon fuels.

But Isn't New Fossil Fuel Being Formed?

Yes, but it is being burned faster than natural forces can create it. Every year about 28 million tons of new fossil sediments are formed, but the world is consuming the present deposits at 200 times that speed. And world consumption is increasing at a rate of 4 percent a year. Also, the population is apparently increasing at a rate that could lead to a doubling of the world's population by the year 2013.

Even if population growth is slowed through birth control, and energy consumption is made less wasteful, sooner or later— in tens of thousands of years—we are going to run out of fossil fuels. And if our careless use of them continues, other irreversible damage will be done. Water systems will fail from pollution. Fertile soil will be poisoned and will deteriorate to sterile desert.

R. GARDNER - 1780 - 1978

Will Alternative Energy Systems
Fill in the Gap?

Perhaps. It is hard to say for sure at present. Many experts feel that the only way we can supply the vast amounts of energy currently demanded by our machines is to further develop high-technology, alternative systems. Others argue that we should emphasize low-technology systems.

What Is Meant by High and Low
Technology?

The simpler alternative systems, called *passive, soft,* or *low technology* (low-tech), require less initial investment and produce less pollution, but they also produce less energy. Generally speaking, they are more adaptable to particular small-scale use in individual homes and small industries. The more complex systems, called *active, hard,* or *high technology* (high-tech), require enormous investment and maintenance, but produce much more energy. They are more productive if used on a larger scale to provide power for communities and large industries.

Some experts believe that low-tech solar, wind, and water alternative systems will be free and easy. The power of the wind, sun, rivers, and oceans is limitless, they say. The use of them will produce all the power we need and will not produce pollutants to further poison our world. But in many cases, this "free and clean" energy is being harvested by building windmills from recycled oil drums and by making solar collectors from glass, copper, steel, aluminum, and plastics. It takes power to heat sand to the melting point to make glass and then roll it out. The mining of metals is done by machines usually run with diesel oil or gasoline. Most plastics are made from coal or petroleum in factories that burn coal, oil, or natural gas, and vent waste products into the air, rivers, or lakes.

Should We Be Discouraged?

No. We are attempting only to point out that our problems are complex and interrelated. Our solutions will involve a great deal more study and work and will probably eventually require an integration of all systems, simple and complex, hard and soft, high-tech and low-tech, coupled with unceasing efforts toward efficiency and conservation—which is not to say that it cannot be done. In fact, if you will turn to the next chapter and read a few pages, you will be able to begin harvesting the sun's (almost) clean and free energy right now.

Fig. 6

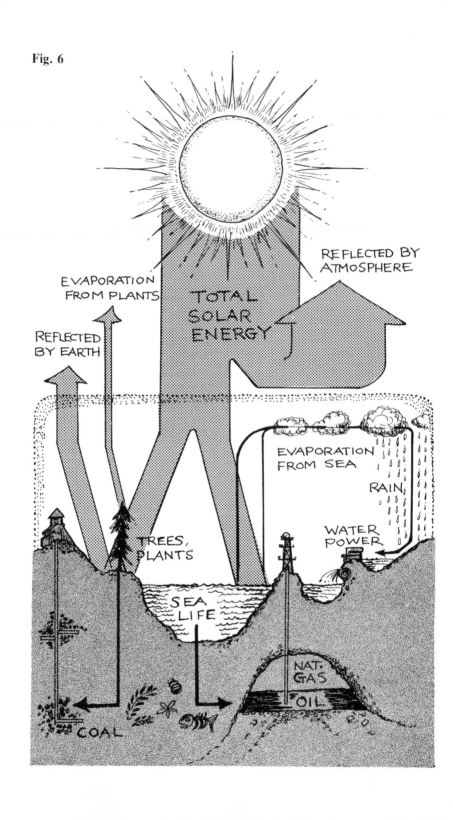

2
SOLAR POWER

What Is Solar Power?

All of our known energy comes initially from the sun. The sun heats the earth and, through the photosynthetic combination of water and atmospheric carbon dioxide, causes plants to grow. Animals and humans eat the plants and derive physical energy. Trees are burned for heat. When some trees fall, they are often buried under tons of earth and rocks and are eventually transformed by pressure and heat into the carbonaceous fossil fuels: coal, oil, and the volatile gases; and pitchblend from which uranium is extracted. The sun's heat causes water to evaporate and be transported through the atmosphere, where it eventually falls as rain or snow. This causes lakes to fill and rivers to flow with enough force to move waterwheels. The alternation of the sun's heat with the night's cold causes shifting air currents that make windmills turn. The sun, in combination with the moon, draws the great oceans to and fro, creating the tides that move wave-propelled machines. In this sense, all energy is solar energy. However, we will limit this chapter to man-made means of exploiting the sun's energy through intervention—the collection of energy by catching or diverting the sun's energy for immediate use or for storage.

Is Solar Power a New Idea?

Not at all. Prehistoric man preferred a cave with its opening toward the winter sun, and 2,400 years ago the Greek Xenophon wrote that a house would be warmer if it faced the sun. Farmers have been using the sun's rays to dry crops since the beginning of agriculture. In 1774 Joseph Priestley concentrated the rays of the sun on mercuric oxide and discovered oxygen. In that same year, the French chemist, Lavoisier, used huge glass lenses to gather concentrated sunlight for his experiments with combustion. The sun's rays have long been used to distill fresh water from salt water, and in 1872 a giant solar still, covering 51,000 square feet of land, was built in Chile. It produced 6,000 gallons of fresh water each day for 40 years.

Solar water heaters appeared in Florida in the early 1800s, and by the 1920s, thousands of the heaters were operating in the southwestern United States, until cheap electricity became available. (As the price of electricity soars, solar water heaters are making a comeback.) The first homes heated by solar energy were built by the Massachusetts Institute of Technology (MIT) in 1939. Twenty years later, Harry Thomason erected the first commercial solar-heated homes in Washington, D.C.

How Much Solar Power Is Available?

The energy that falls on a single sunbather in the form of sunlight in the course of a day could power a home for a week—*if* all that power could be collected. In a single year, our planet receives 1.5 million trillion horsepower-hours of energy from the sun. But most of that energy is bounced back into the atmosphere by a process called *thermal radiation*, as shown in Figure 6. It is this reflection, or radiation of energy back into space, that keeps the earth from overheating and saves us from being burned to a crisp.

How Much of That Energy Can Be Put to Use?

Of the solar energy that does reach the earth's surface, we

can convert about 10 percent into electricity and about 50 percent into heat for a house.

How Is It Done?

Solar energy is converted by using glass or other such transparent materials to exploit a phenomenon known as "the greenhouse effect." Energy from the sun passes through space as

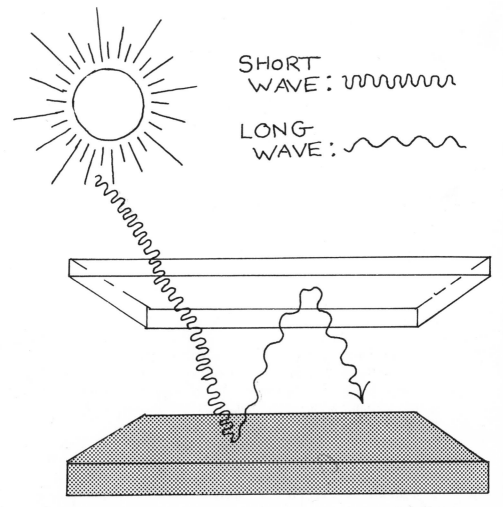

SHORT WAVE:

LONG WAVE:

Fig. 7

radiant energy, most of it shortwave, visible light. When this energy strikes an object, such as a piece of plywood, a portion is absorbed by the plywood and transformed into *thermal* or *heat energy*. Heat energy produces a rapid motion of atoms and molecules within the plywood. But the plywood almost immediately absorbs the rays, converts them to longwave thermal energy, and begins to radiate that energy outward again. You can test this by putting your hand in front of a sun-heated piece of plywood or metal. The heat you feel is thermal radiation.

How can you prevent the heat from being lost through thermal radiation? If you put a pane of glass in front of the plywood, you will find that the energy loss is immediately reduced. The reason for this is because glass transmits shortwave radiation but also absorbs longwave radiation, trapping the heat behind the glass—inside the "greenhouse." This greenhouse effect, illustrated in Figure 7, is what makes a car become hot after it has been left in the sun with the windows rolled up.

How Can the Greenhouse Effect Be Tested?

By making an instant solar collector.

HOW TO MAKE AN INSTANT SOLAR COLLECTOR

You will need a sunny winter day (summer will do, but the results will not be as impressive) and a one-gallon glass jar. A translucent, plastic jug in which milk is sold may be used, but plastics do not absorb thermal radiation as well as glass. A thermometer will help you test the results.

Fill one-half of the jar with water, cap it, and place it on the inside sill of a window pane that faces the sun, usually on the south side of the house. A single pane will do, but if there is also a storm window pane, that will increase the effectiveness of your thermal radiation trap. Within an hour or two on a clear, sunny

Fig. 8

day, the outside of the jar above the water level should feel warm
to the touch. If you remove the cap and put your finger in the
jar, you will find that the air above the water is even warmer.
This is because the shortwave solar rays have entered through
the layers of glass and have been transformed into thermal
energy in the air and water inside the jar, as shown in Figure 8.
This thermal energy then tries to radiate outward, but most of it
is trapped by the glass.

Using your thermometer, measure the temperature of the
wall just outside the window. Then measure the inside room
temperature and the temperature of the air inside the jar. If it is
noon or thereabouts, and the house has been centrally heated
the previous night, the temperature inside the house will be
higher than the temperature outside. But the temperature inside

15

your instant collector will be higher than both. Thanks to glass and the greenhouse effect, you have collected solar energy, converted it to thermal energy, and stored some of it in the water in the jar.

(Late in the afternoon of a summer day, the temperature inside a poorly insulated house might be higher than the outside temperature because the house itself is also a giant collector. But the temperature of the air inside the jar is still likely to be higher than that anywhere else.)

The efficiency of your solar collector can be improved by placing a panel covered with a shiny surfaced material, such as aluminum foil, outside the window. It should be tilted so as to reflect the sunlight and direct extra shortwave radiation to the window and jar. See Solar Greenhouse, Figure 14, for the construction of a reflecting panel.

The efficiency of your collector will be further improved by placing a blackened absorber panel of wood or metal *behind* the jar. As nightfall approaches and the outside and inside house temperatures drop, you will notice that the water in the jar continues to be warmer than the surrounding air. This means you have succeeded in not only collecting solar energy, but in storing it. A fan could then be used to move the air past the jar between it and the window pane, drawing off that stored energy and carrying it elsewhere to help warm colder areas of the house.

Why Should the Absorber Panel Be Black?

Because blackened surfaces do a better job of converting shortwave radiation to longwave thermal radiation than light-colored surfaces. Rough surfaces also do a better job than smooth surfaces.

Why Should the Energy Be Stored?

It is necessary to store the energy because the sun shines only during the day, but heating needs continue through the night. One of the main stumbling blocks to the effective use of solar energy is the fact that there is often an overabundance of sunshine when it is not needed, and none at all when it is most needed. To solve this problem, we must first understand the way in which heat moves or flows.

Heat, or thermal energy, always flows from warm areas to cooler areas. The rate of movement is proportional to the temperature difference between the source of the heat and the object or area to which it is flowing. If there were no interference by air currents resulting from the warming of day and the cooling of night, everything would eventually be the same temperature. Heat always flows in a direction that will equalize temperatures.

How Does Heat Flow?

Heat flows by three methods: conduction, convection, and radiation.

Fig. 9

Conduction is the flow of heat through solid materials. When a stove heats an iron skillet, heat from the burner flows up through the pan and out toward the end of the handle, always moving from the hotter area to the colder. The heat is conducted by the metal. Copper conducts heat better than iron because it takes less heat to warm it and also because it has greater *conductance*. In other words, copper has less resistance to heat flow than iron.

Convection is heat flow through the movement of fluids. Both liquids and gases are considered to be fluids. In a kettle on a stove, water is first heated at the bottom. It then rises and mixes with the cooler water above, spreading the heat and warming the entire volume of water more quickly than could have been done by conduction alone. The same phenomenon occurs with air, which is a combination of gases. When a furnace heats air in a basement, the warm air rises by convection to the living areas, traveling, as heat always does, from warm to cooler places.

Heated fluids also tend to expand and rise. Convection of heated fluids can be natural or forced. In natural convection, a fluid is warmed, and becomes less dense. Because a fluid's gyrating molecules are further apart, the fluid is buoyant in the surrounding, cooler fluid. So it rises, while the cooler fluid that flows in to replace it is heated in turn. If the already warmed fluid (water or gas) moves by natural convection to a cooler place, its heat is then absorbed by the cooler surroundings. It then cools again, becomes heavier, and sinks.

This circular process of heating, expanding, rising, con-vective movement to a cooler place, followed by the cooling, shrinking, and sinking of the fluid, is called *thermosiphoning*. It works because of convection. For an example, see the solar greenhouse, Figures 12, 13 and 14.

Forced convection is simply the speeding up of the con-vection process by using a pump or blower to move the heated fluid along faster.

In summary, conduction is the flow of heat through solid materials. Convection is flow of heat through the movement of fluids such as water or air. Radiation is the flow of heat through open space. In Figure 9, there is radiation into the room from the sun through the window, from the skillet handle, and from the stove. There is conduction from the frying pan to the handle and from the metal bottom of the kettle to the water inside it. There is convection via the air-fluid moving around the stove and the steam hissing from the kettle.

These three kinds of heat flow can be put to work to collect, move, and store solar energy for the heating of a house. Solar heating systems can be divided into two categories: passive and active.

What Are Passive and Active Heating Systems?

Generally speaking, a *passive solar system* uses little or no mechanical devices to move heated air. *Active solar systems* use fans and blowers to move heated air to cooler areas or to a storage area. Passive systems are soft or low-technology systems. Active systems are hard or high-tech systems.

In the basic passive system, the sun's rays are encouraged to penetrate directly into a home, and the thermal energy is kept there by the simplest possible means. The aim is to make the house itself a collector of solar energy, a storehouse of solar energy, and a heat trap to keep in the energy. Most houses do this to some extent, and most houses can be improved as passive or direct systems. But a good passive system requires careful positioning, or orientation, of the house to the sun. The best passive systems also require special construction techniques.

How Do You Orient a House or Solar Collector to the Sun?

By carefully locating the house so it effectively receives the sun's rays. As you have noticed, the sun travels in a circular path across the sky each day, reaching its highest point at noon. It rises in the east and travels in an east-west direction and sets close to due west. It rises later in winter than in summer, its path is lower, and it sets earlier. As winter proceeds into spring and summer, the sun's circular path moves higher in the sky, and it begins to rise earlier and set later, as shown in Figure 10. (The

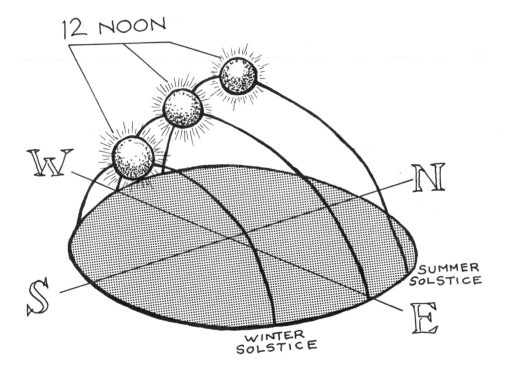

Fig. 10

winter solstice is that point at which fall passes into winter, about December 21. The summer solstice is that point at which spring passes into summer, about June 21.)

Any solar system will work efficiently when its collecting surface is at exact right angles to the sun's rays at all times. This is made more difficult by the fact that the angle of the sun's rays changes hour by hour throughout each day, and day by day throughout the year. Lighter solar collectors can be equipped with machinery to make them move with the movement of the sun; they can always face it at the proper angle.

Speaking generally for the continental United States, the collecting surface should face due south and be tilted at an angle of from 50° to 60° from horizontal, as is the collecting surface of the glass windows in the basic house shown in Figure 11.

What Special Construction Techniques Are Needed for a Passive System?

The average home is designed to be heated mostly from the inside. But a solar home should be designed to be heated from the outside in. This means that it must first get the solar energy in, and then hold it for as long as possible. Just as heat can be gained by radiation, conduction, and convection, it can be lost by the same means. A house with a well-constructed passive system has a large window area to take in thermal radiation, and thick walls, insulated on the outside, to retard outward thermal loss.

Figure 11 shows a basic passive-system solar house. Note that there are no pumps, blowers, or other moving parts. Aside

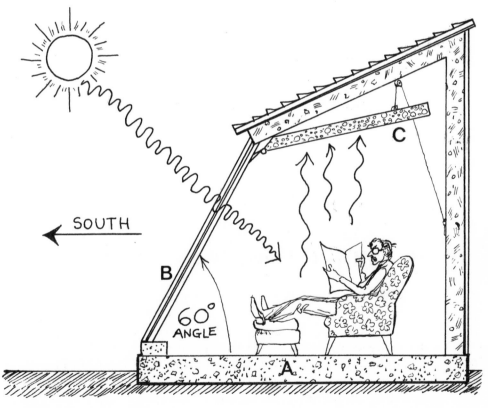

Fig. 11

from the cost of construction, the heating is virtually maintenance free, and uses no electric or fossil fuel power. The floor is a concrete slab 8 to 12 inches thick. The walls are also of thick concrete, insulated on the outside. The large window area, *B*, faces due south at a 60° angle to the horizontal, and has double panes of glass. The sun's rays enter through the glass and are trapped inside as thermal radiation due to the greenhouse effect. Thus, during the day, the house acts as a giant solar collector. Once the heat is collected, it is prevented from returning through the walls because of their thickness and the fact that they are insulated on the outside. These walls absorb and store the heat, contributing to what is called the *thermal mass* of the house: its heat-storage capacity. At nightfall, once there is no more solar energy to collect, the shutter, *C*, is lowered to close off the windows and retard heat loss. In an ideal passive system, this stored heat would be sufficient to warm the interior until more thermal energy becomes available at sunrise.

How Can You Test a Passive Solar System for Yourself?

By building a passive-system solar greenhouse.

HOW TO BUILD A PASSIVE-SYSTEM SOLAR GREENHOUSE

An inexpensive, free-standing A-frame greenhouse is particularly effective for getting spring seedlings started in cold climates. These instructions are for a greenhouse with a floor area measuring 10′ × 12′ (120 square feet). A smaller version can be built with only two of the three sections shown in Figure 12. A larger version might use ten-foot 2″ × 4″ stud-uprights instead of the eight-footers shown.

For the wooden frame you will need:

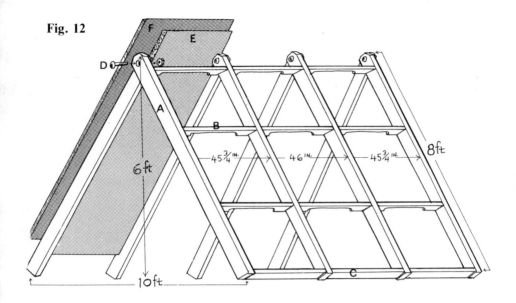

Fig. 12

8	8-foot lengths of 2″ × 4″ lumber (Second grade lumber will do for both slopes, unless you plan to glaze the structure with old windows, see below.)
8	45¾″ lengths of 1″ × 4″ lumber
4	46″ lengths of 1″ × 4″ lumber
3	8′ × 4′ sheets of plywood (Exterior lumber is best, but interior will do if you plan to cover the rear slope with roofing.)
4	5″ carriage or stove bolts with nuts and washers assorted lumber for framing the ends

The north or rear slope of the greenhouse is closed to weather and sun, while the south or front slope is double-glazed to admit the sun's rays. Four combinations of glazing (installation of glass panes) are possible: (1) two layers of glass, (2) two layers of Teflon or other plastic film, (3) an outer layer of Sun-Lite or other sheet plastic, an inner layer of plastic film, (4) an outer layer of old windows, an inner layer of plastic film.

See page 35 for a comparison of glass, sheet plastic, and plastic films. Keep in mind that if you use old windows, you may have to adjust the dimensions of the frame to accommodate their particular dimensions. To insure a snug fit for windows, you must buy good quality, straight 2″ × 4″ stud-uprights.

Our greenhouse uses glazing combination (3), for which you will need:

117   square feet of 4-mil Teflon or other clear plastic film
3   4′ × 8′ panels of Sun-Lite (See Kalwall Corporation in the Appendix under Suppliers) or other translucent plastic sheeting
8   8′ lengths of wood lathe or other light lumber

For best results, insulate the rear north slope and add an inside reflective surface, for which you will need:

3   4′ × 8′ sheets of 1″ styrofoam insulation
2   100-square-foot rolls of aluminum foil or other reflecting surface (See the Appendix under Suppliers.)

Finally, you will need the usual carpentry tools plus a heavy-duty staple gun and a box of T-50 ⅜″ 9.52 mm staples, available at most hardware stores.

Before assembling the frame, select a site that is smooth, level, and well drained. Mark out rough floor dimensions on the ground, making sure you orient the south slope toward the sun as it stands at midday. If you plan to mount the greenhouse on a foundation, it must be prepared before the frame is erected. (See page 22).

To assemble the frame, first drill a hole in the end of each 8′ 2 × 4 (*A*, Figure 12) to accommodate the bolts, *D*, Figure 12. Round off the same end of each 2 × 4 upright with a saw so that the peak of the greenhouse will have a smooth apex. Assemble four pairs of the 2 × 4s to form the series of inverted "V"'s, as shown in Figure 12. You will need help setting them upright as shown. To keep them in place until the rear wall can be nailed on, tack scrap lumber holding-strips along the front face. Next, nail the sheets of plywood, one by one, to the rear slope, as shown, *F*. (*E* is the foam insulation, which will later be added from the inside.) Take the two outside plywood panels right to the edge of the outside 2 × 4 uprights. That will leave ¾″ on each of the center uprights for support of the third, middle plywood panel. Firmly nail the panels in place. A bead of latex caulking compound, laid down the length of each upright before nailing, will insure a tight air seal between uprights and plywood panels.

Now the 1″ × 4″ spacers can be added to the front slope, as shown, B, Figure 12. All of the spacers can be solid like those at the bottom, C. Or, those above the bottom level can be cut before mounting, as shown, B. These crescent cuts will allow a chimney, or flue-like effect, between the two layers of glazing so that the air that is heated between the glazing can rise by convection and thermosiphoning. This will result in a continual circulation and reheating of the air, as indicated in Figure 15, B.

The spacers can be toe-nailed directly to the 2 × 4 uprights, or they can be made more secure with mounting blocks (see F, Figure 14).

Frame the two ends of the greenhouse to suit your taste. The east end should have a door opening (B, Figure 13). The opposite west end can be framed with similar uprights and will be glazed solid. You can make a door frame and hinge it to the upright, B, or you can simply hang a double or triple layer of plastic film as a door flap, nailing a strip of lathe along the bottom to give it weight.

Make sure all uprights are seated firmly on the ground and that all angles are true. Now, you are ready to add the glazing.

Figure 13 shows how the panels of Sun-Lite or other plastic

Fig. 13

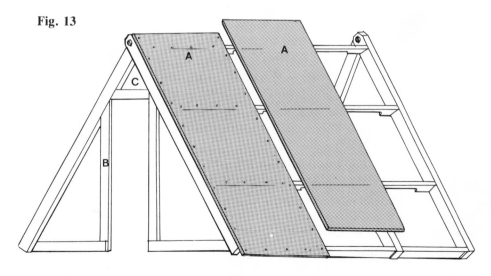

25

glazing, *A,* are positioned on the outside surface of the south slope and nailed in place. If you lay a bead of caulking compound before nailing, you have a better air seal. More caulking can be added to seal the cracks between panels, and water-resistant tape can be added to further improve the seal. If you are using old windows for outside glazing, they should also be well caulked. If you are using plastic film for outside glazing, staple it in place as shown, *E,* in the middle diagram of Figure 14. Lathe should then be nailed over the film to hold it in place, *D.*

Once the outside glazing is in place, add the inside sheet of Teflon or other film. This is stapled to the inside edges of the uprights and spacers, starting at one end and pulling the film taut as you go. Secure the inside glazing by nailing on strips of lathe, as shown for the outside (center of Figure 14).

You now have your south or front slopes glazed inside and out with a double layer of transparent material. If you have used the specially cut spacers shown in Figure 12, *B,* you may now cut narrow slots in the bottom and top of the inside glazing panels, as indicated in Figure 15, *A-b.* These vent openings will encourage the thermosiphoning circulation of air that is indicated in the bottom diagram, *B,* of Figure 15.

Both ends of the greenhouse should also be double-glazed with one of the suggested combinations of material. The simplest method is to staple double layers of film to the end framing, trying to leave at least two inches of air space between the layers. A vent should be provided at one end for fresh air circulation *(C,* Figure 13). This vent can be provided with its own small door or can be hung with a double flap of film.

The peak must be finished with a runner cut from heavy tar paper or metal flashing, as shown in *A,* center of Figure 14. This should overlap all openings at the peak and should be cemented and nailed to the rear slope. If you decide to add the reflecting panels (top of Figure 14, *C),* the leading edge of the peak runner should be left loose so that when the reflecting panels are raised at night, their top edges can be tucked under the runner flap, as indicated, *A,* top of Figure 14. If there are no reflecting panels, cement and nail the runner securely along the top of the front slope as well.

Seal the bottom edges of the greenhouse by heaping earth all around the bottom of the structure and tamping it down so

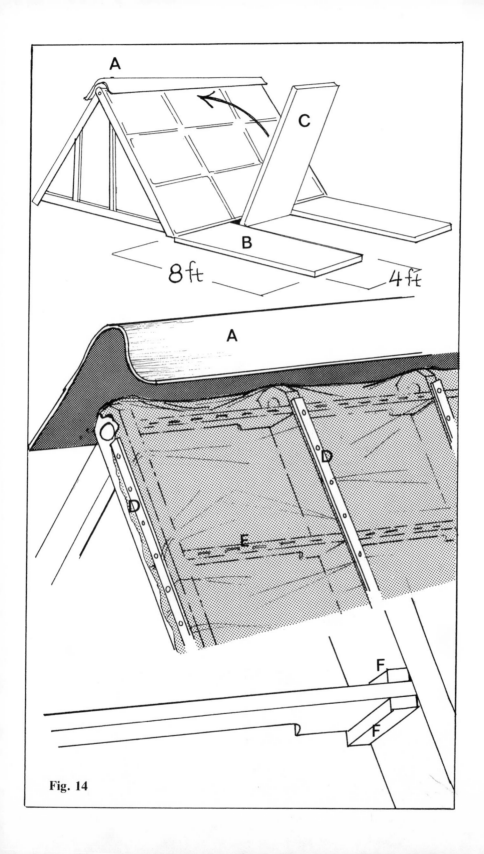

Fig. 14

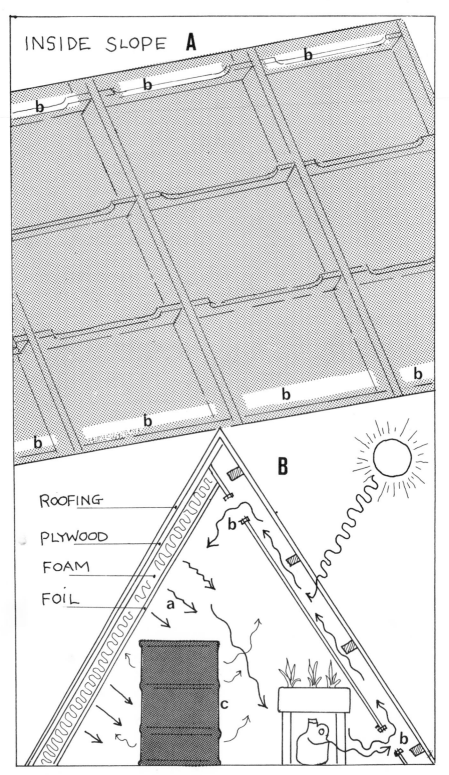

INSIDE SLOPE **A**

B

ROOFING
PLYWOOD
FOAM
FOIL

Fig. 15

that all air gaps are well sealed. The surface of the rear slope can be further sealed with a covering of stapled film, tar paper, or asphalt roofing.

To better insulate the rear slope from north winds, add the styrofoam panels (*E*, Figure 12) to the inside of the rear wall, securing them between the uprights with the special cement provided for that purpose by most hardware stores. Aluminum foil can then be cemented and stapled over this inside insulation to provide a reflecting surface that will direct incoming sun rays down onto the planters and water storage drums (*B-a*, Figure 15).

The volume of heat storage to be included inside the greenhouse depends on how much room you can spare from the space needed for your plants. We used four 3′ steel drums, painted black to better absorb the thermal energy. The drums were filled with water and arranged in a row under the rear slope, as indicated, *b*, Figure 16, and *B-c*, Figure 16. A plank was then placed across the tops of the drums, and a row of water-filled plastic jugs was lined up on top of the plank, *A-c*, Figure 16. We also stacked other jugs and beer cans, filled with water, in all the unused nooks and crannies. The greater the volume of water inside the greenhouse, the better the heat storage and the longer it will maintain a warm temperature through the night.

The reflecting panels indicated in *B* and *C*, top of Figure 14, serve two purposes. Their upper surfaces are coated with aluminum foil to help bounce more solar energy into the greenhouse, and they are hinged at the bottom so that they can be raised at night, *C*, to cover the glazed front slope and to help prevent the stored heat from radiating through the glazing. Make them from ¼″ plywood, preferably with a 2″ layer of styrofoam insulation cemented to the inside surface. The reflecting foil should then be cemented to the styrofoam.

For further heat absorption inside the greenhouse, and to help in the conversion of shortwave radiation into longwave radiation, paint whatever you can with matte-black, high-absorbency paint. Paint designed especially for this purpose is available from suppliers listed in the Appendix. However, stovepipe paint, sold in hardware stores, is almost as effective and is less expensive. A sheet of black plastic film on the floor also contributes to the shortwave conversion effect, and you can

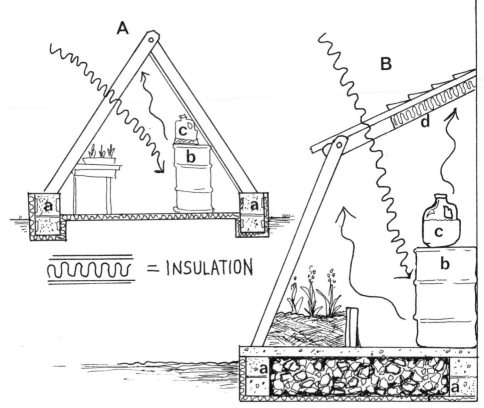

Fig. 16

even paint the back surfaces of your plastic jugs black to make them more effective solar collectors.

Heat storage can be further improved by the addition of a bed of fist-sized rocks under the greenhouse floor, as shown in Diagram *B, (a-a)* Figure 16. A foundation adds considerably to the cost and labor of building a greenhouse, but it also adds to its heat storage capacity. Diagram *A*, Figure 16, suggests a foundation made of cement blocks *(a-a)*, with a 2″ layer of styrofoam insulation added on the outside. A deeper foundation would be even more effective because the earth below the frost line (about 36 inches) always stays at a temperature of above 50° F, regardless of the temperature of the ground surface. Thus, some of the warmth of the earth below a snow-chilled ground will be conducted up through the foundation and into the walls.

The same basic materials used for the A-frame greenhouse can be used to make a lean-to greenhouse like the one suggested, Diagram *B*, Figure 16. The advantage of a lean-to is that it absorbs a certain amount of warmth from the house wall against which it leans. Such a greenhouse must, of course, be placed against the south-facing wall of the house. Note that only one-half of the roof, *B*, is glazed, while the rest, *d*, is roofed and insulated. This is to prevent the direct sunlight of summer days from burning the plants below.

You may want to add an auxiliary heating system to your greenhouse for security against sub-zero temperatures. A small electric heater will do, or you can incorporate a wood or sawdust stove (see page 128).

With your greenhouse completed, you will have built a functioning, passive-direct solar system. Between such fully passive systems and the hi-tech active systems, there are a variety of half-and-half systems that might be termed indirect systems.

How Does an Indirect System Work?

An *indirect system* does not take in solar rays as directly as a completely passive system, so an indirect system often utilizes special water tanks or rock bins for storage of collected heat. An example is shown in Figure 17. This house collects and stores solar energy in a plastic bag of water on the roof, *A*. On a sunny day, the insulating cover, *B*, is opened, and the sun heats the water in the waterbed. At night the cover is closed to keep the heat from radiating upward. The heat is then distributed downward, throughout the sunless night, into the well-insulated house. Such a system can also cool a house in summer by operating the pond or waterbed system in reverse. The insulating cover is kept closed by day so that heat from the room will be absorbed by the water on the roof. At night, the cover is opened, and the heat radiates to the night sky.

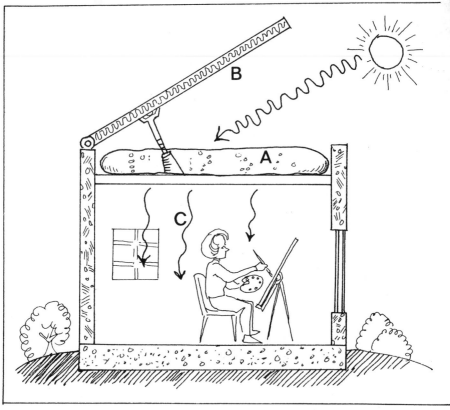

Fig. 17

Are There Other Ways of Storing Solar Heat?

Yes. Heat can be stored in beds of rock like that shown for the lean-to greenhouse in Figure 16, *B*. It can also be stored in gravel, sand, and clay or high-magnesium bricks. Water, however, is a better storage medium than concrete, gravel, or rocks. Water also distributes heat more quickly than concrete, due to convection. And water maintains its heat longer. (Paraffin and special salts are even more efficient storers of heat than water.) Water is also cheaper and more plentiful than the other materials. For these reasons, water is the most common storage medium used in solar systems.

How Do Active, High-Tech Systems Work?

High-tech systems usually use rooftop, flat-plate collectors and separate storage devices. This means that the heated fluid, usually water or air, must be moved from the collection point for storage during the day, and from the storage area to the rest of the house during the night. This requires pipes or ducts to route the fluids, and pumps or fans to move them along. But, in order to harvest and store the solar energy, other energy must be expended (usually electricity) to drive the pumps or fans. For this reason, active systems are considered hard, or high-tech, systems.

Figure 18 shows a basic, indirect active system, using water

Fig. 18

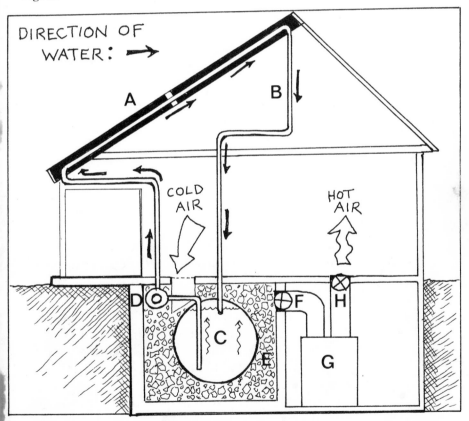

as the collecting and storage medium and air as the delivery fluid. The solar collectors, A, located on the roof, heat water. The water then drains, B, into the storage tank, C, located in the basement. The hotter water in the tank rises to the top by convection, while the cooler water in the bottom is forced by the pump, D, up to the collectors on the roof, where it is heated and again drained downward, B, into the tank. In the meantime, the heat from the water in the tank is being transferred by conduction to the rocks surrounding the tank, E, and to the air spaces between the rocks. When a thermostat indicates that heat is needed in the rooms above, a blower, F, sucks the hot air out of the rock bed, through the auxiliary heater, G, up through another blower, H, and into the rooms above.

Note that a pump and two blowers are needed, both run by electricity. The auxiliary heater is run by oil, electricity, or coal. Most solar systems require this kind of backup heater to maintain efficiency on cloudy days. An actual operating system might need even more complicated machinery, all consuming energy, in need of maintenance, and subject to breakdown.

How Does a Flat-plate Collector Work?

A flat-plate collector exploits the greenhouse effect. Basically, it is a scaled-down version of our passive-system greenhouse, equipped with a means of causing unheated fluid to flow in and heated fluid to flow out. The fluid can be air or water or it can be water with an anti-freeze solution added to prevent it from freezing in cold weather. As shown in the diagram, Figure 19, the collector consists of one or more glass or plastic cover plates, A, with a black absorber panel, B, behind the glass. There is insulation, E, behind the absorber to retard heat loss. (In the completed collector, all of these components are contained in a wood or metal box or a pan.) The transparent cover plates collect and trap the light. The transfer fluid enters the header pipe, C, and flows out of the holes and down across the face of the absorber, while gaining heat by conduction from the hot absorber panel. The trough at the bottom collects the heated water and takes it via the pipe, D, to the rest of the system. The collector shown trickles water directly down the channeled or

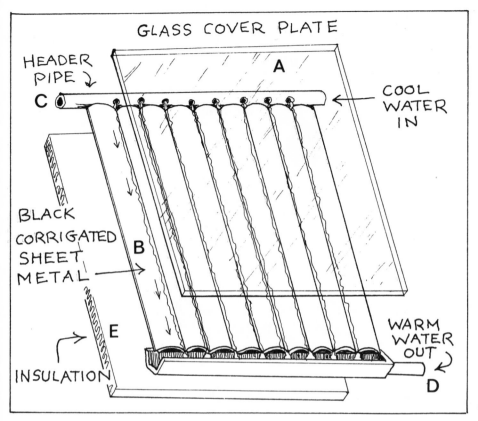

GLASS COVER PLATE

HEADER PIPE ↘

A

C

COOL WATER IN

BLACK CORRIGATED SHEET METAL →

B

WARM WATER OUT ↘

E

D

INSULATION

Fig. 19

corrugated surface of the absorber. Other collectors pass the fluid through pipes affixed to the face of the absorber plate, see Figure 23.

What Materials Should Be Used for the Collector Cover Plate?

Glass is best. Two or more panes will trap the thermal energy better than a single pane. Although plastic is cheaper and easier to work with than glass, almost all plastics deteriorate after exposure to ultraviolet rays. Thin plastic film can be used for the second, inside cover plate if glass is used on the outside. Sun-Lite, a fiberglass-reinforced polyester made by the Kalwall Corporation (see Appendix), has a good solar transmittance and is easy to work with. However, it should never be used as the inner cover of a two-pane collector, only as the outside cover.

What Material Should Be Used for the Absorber Plate?

If the collecting fluid is air, almost any dark-surfaced material can be used, even painted cardboard or dark cotton gauze. Liquid-system collectors usually have metal absorber plates. Copper, galvanized sheet iron, and aluminum absorb heat well, but copper is expensive and aluminum corrodes.

Absorber surfaces should be dull black. (See the Appendix for special paints that produce high-absorbency selective surfaces). Flat black stovepipe paint does nearly as well.

Insulation should be fiberglass or mineral wool because styrofoam and urethane insulations tend to break down at high temperatures.

How Are Liquid-system Collectors Used?

They are used for home space heating (see Figure 18) and are especially effective for heating water. If the sun is shining outside, you can heat water within a few hours by making an instant solar water heater.

HOW TO MAKE AN INSTANT SOLAR WATER HEATER

You will need a black, rubber watering hose, attached to an outside faucet, as shown in Figure 20. Place the hose on the lawn under the sun. The sun will heat the outer surface of the hose, causing the heat to migrate to the water inside by conduction. By adjusting the faucet, you can have a steady stream of warm-to-hot water as long as the sun is shining.

Other simple solar water heaters are shown in Figure 21. In

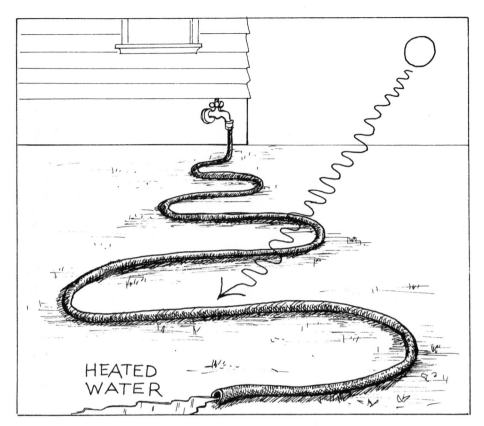

HEATED
WATER

Fig. 20

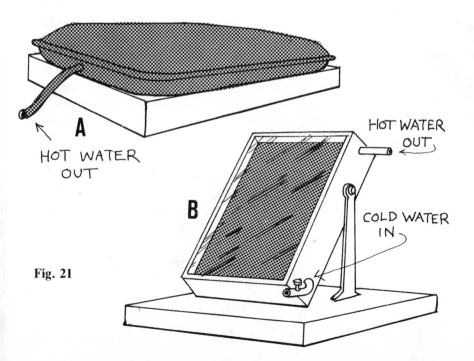

A

HOT WATER
OUT

B

HOT WATER
OUT

COLD WATER
IN

Fig. 21

Japan, the hot water needs of many households are met by a simple black, plastic bag water heater, such as the one shown, *A*. The bag is filled in the morning and drained in the evening. Heating efficiency can be increased by placing the bag in a shallow, insulated box and stretching a transparent cover across it. Such horizontal, flat-basin collectors work best in the tropics, where the sun is high overhead most of the year. When the sun is lower in the horizon, the collector must be raised from the horizontal in order to catch the direct rays of the sun. The simple upright collector shown, *B*, consists of a closed-box tank darkened on its facing surface to absorb solar radiation, and with a sheet of glass to take advantage of the greenhouse effect. Cold water enters at the bottom and rises by convection as it heats. It is then drawn off at the top. You can make either of these hot water heaters with common tools and materials.

The water from such collectors can be used for bathing, drinking, or cooking. But in regions where temperatures drop below freezing, ice would soon burst the pipes of these heaters, so wherever there is risk of freezing, an anti-freeze solution must be included in the water. *Note:* ANTI-FREEZE IS A DEADLY POISON.

Figure 22 illustrates how the heating fluid can be kept separate from the drinking water. The common method is by using a *heat exchanger*. The heating medium, with its deadly anti-freeze mixture, is contained entirely inside a closed loop of pipe. In the version shown, the anti-freeze mixture travels upward through the collector, *A*. It is then driven downward by the pump, *B*, into a coil contained inside a tank of water. The coil, *C*, is the heat exchanger. It heats the water in the tank by conduction, and the safe drinking water can then be drawn off, *D*.

The construction of such a system is beyond the scope of this book, but you can produce hot water for bathing (and for drinking and cooking, if you do not include anti-freeze) by building your own thermosiphoning solar water heater.

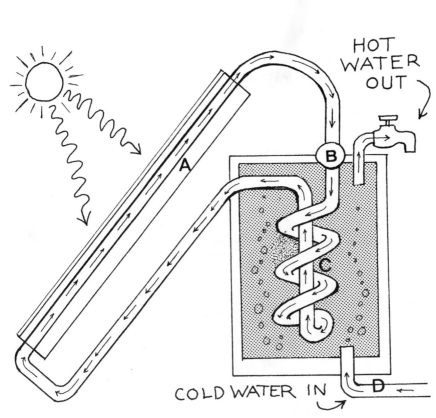

HOT WATER OUT

A

B

C

COLD WATER IN

D

Fig. 22

HOW TO BUILD A THERMOSIPHONING SOLAR WATER HEATER

The water heater (Figure 23) consists of a flat-plate collector, *B*, and a storage can, *A*, connected to form a closed loop, with a separate hose, *b*, for delivering new water to the system. Don't let all these pipes discourage you. Once you understand how it works, construction is relatively simple. Parts are available at any large hardware store, and the heater can be put together with ordinary hand tools. Here is how it works: The sun strikes the glass-covered face of the collector and heats the metal

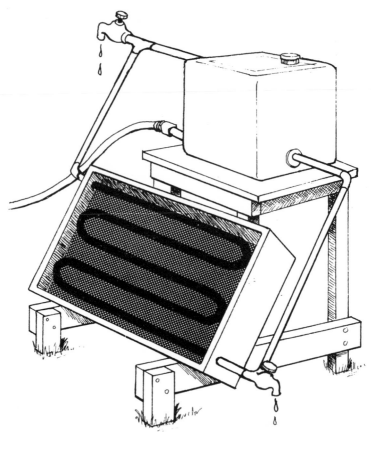

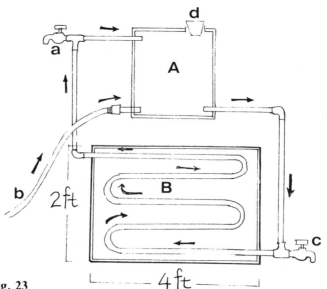

a

d

A

b

2 ft

B

C

4 ft

Fig. 23

absorber plate, which uses conduction to heat the water inside the pipe coil. Convection causes the hotter water to rise up the coil and into the top of the collection tank. At the top, there is a faucet, *a,* for drawing off hot water. The cold water at the bottom of the tank flows downward into the bottom of the coil, where it is reheated inside the collector. The water then rises again to continue the thermosiphoning cycle. At the bottom of the cold water drainage tube, there is a second faucet, *c,* for draining the system in cold weather and for draining off sediment that might clog the system.

The storage can shown is a five-gallon gasoline can, but a larger and heavier tank can be used. On sunny spring days, the system can heat up to 50 gallons. Our version uses flexible pipe inside the collector because it is easier to bend into the serpentine shape of the coil, but the coil could be made from rigid pipe and corner fittings "sweated," or soldered, together. We used rigid pipe and fittings for the delivery and drainage loops, but they can also be made from flexible pipe or even from rubber or plastic hose.

First, let's make the collector. The collector, *A,* Figure 24, consists of a wooden box containing a "sandwich" of a glass cover plate, *a,* an absorber plate, *b,* an inside backing panel, *c,* a space for insulation, *d,* and a rear panel. The copper coil is soldered to the face of the absorber plate, as indicated by the dotted lines, *A,* Figure 24.

To make the collector, you will need:

1   22½" × 46½" sheet single-weight window glass or Sun-Lite plastic

1   21½" × 45½" sheet ⅛" copper plate or galvanized iron (Copper is the best absorber, but galvanized iron is cheaper.)

22   feet of ½" flexible copper pipe (Make sure you get the soft, malleable type sold from rolls.)

12   feet of 1" × 8" good grade lumber or plywood

1   22½" × 46½" panel of ½" plywood

1   2' × 4' panel of 2½" fiberglass insulation, foil-backed, solder and soldering equipment, caulking compound, metal punch, nails, hammer, saw, scrap lumber

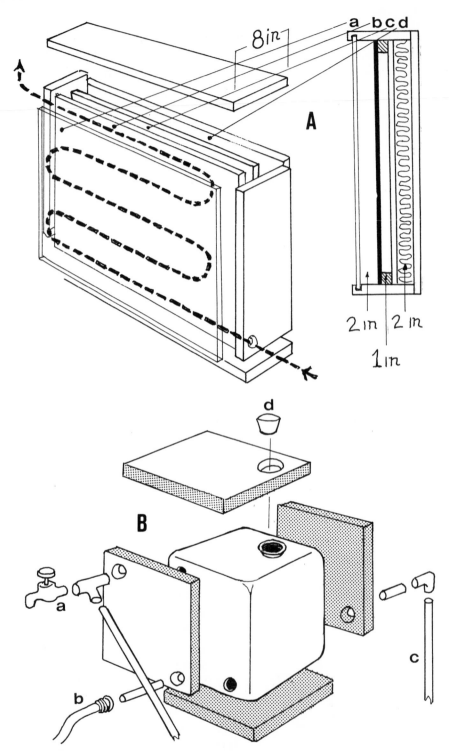

8in

a b c d

2in   2in

1in

A

d

B

a

b

c

Fig. 24

The absorber plate should be put together first. Thoroughly clean the sheet of copper or iron, by sanding away corrosion or paint, if necessary. Then use a pencil to draw the serpentine shape of the coil on its face. Straighten the 22' length of flexible copper pipe and clean it, then begin to bend it into the coil shape, using the pencil pattern on the plate as a guide. Start by leaving six inches of pipe extending beyond the top left-hand corner of the plate. (This will later extend outside the box.) Take your time forming the coil, and be sure not to squeeze or pinch the pipe as it bends. Try to keep the parallel loops equi-distant from one another. Make the coil as flat as possible so that it will fit snugly against the face of the plate along its full length. Place it on the face of the plate so that the upper left end extends beyond that corner and the other end extends six inches beyond the lower right-hand corner. Cut off any excess.

Now solder the coil to the face of the plate. Clamp the plate to a flat surface to prevent it from curling under the heat of the torch or soldering iron. A narrow board, laid diagonally across the coil, will help to hold it in position and flat against the plate as you work. A small propane torch is handiest for the soldering, but a soldering iron will do. Or, you can have the soldering done at a machine shop. Spot solder about every six inches, making sure the coil touches the plate along its full length for good conduction.

Clean coil and plate again, then paint the whole absorber face and tubes with a flat, black paint such as stovepipe paint. Finally, position wooden chocks, or lengths of lumber, behind the plate and nail them to it. They should be cut to hold the plate exactly one inch from the inside backing panel as shown, upper right, A, Figure 24.

Now prepare the parts for the box. Cut the lengths of 1" × 8" lumber to form the four sides of the box. If possible, rout slots in the 1 × 8s along the front inside edges to receive the glass. (This can be done at a wood-working shop.) If you do not rout the grooves, secure the glass with light strips of wood. Complete the box following the diagram, A, Figure 24. Note that a 2" space is required between the glass cover plate and the absorber plate, a 1" gap between the absorber plate and the inside backing panel, and a 2" space for the insulation. Install the insulation with its aluminum foil face toward the inside backing panel. Caulk or glue all joints for an air-tight seal, and take particular care to seal all around the edges of the glass cover plate. (Double-glazing is more effective than single, but you will have to make adaptations in the box design to accommodate a second glass plate.)

Next, assemble the delivery and drain pipe loops and the storage tank. For this you will need:

1	five-gallon metal can with a removable top
9	feet of ½″ rigid copper pipe
2	"sweat"-type ½″ copper elbow joints
2	"sweat"-type ½″ copper T-joints
1	female garden hose connection and fittings
2	faucets of the "sweat," or solder, type. (If only threaded faucets are available, you will have to buy appropriate adapters and bushings for attaching the faucets. Consult your hardware dealer, showing him the diagrams.)
1	rubber stopper to fit the storage tank's top opening
6	sheets 1″ styrofoam insulation measured to fit the six sides of the storage can

Clean the storage can thoroughly—several times if it has been used to store a toxic substance such as gasoline. Next, make the appropriate openings to accommodate the tubing: two holes in one side and a single hole on the opposite side. Use a metal punch instead of a drill because a punch will push inward and produce a flange for better soldering of the intake and outlet pipes. Work carefully, gradually enlarging the holes until they are no more than ½″ in diameter. Then place the collector and tank in position, as shown in Figure 23. Use a table or sawhorses to make sure that the bottom of the tank is to the rear of the collector and at least six inches higher than the top edge of the collector. Loosely assemble the parts of both loops to get the angles right, leaving out the faucets. When you are satisfied that the parts will meet and close correctly all around, disassemble them enough to allow the six panels of styrofoam insulation to be slipped into place, as shown, *B,* Figure 24. Cement the foam to the sides of the can to form an insulating, outer envelope. Then begin "sweating," or soldering, the loops together, starting with the lower right-hand intake pipe. Enlist the help of an extra pair of hands to hold the parts in place while you work. Once the loops are completed, the faucets (*a* and *c*) can be added, and then the garden hose connection for the water intake loop, *b*, Figures 23 and 24. Run water from the garden hose into the system to make sure there are no leaks.

Finally, insert the rubber stopper into the top opening of the storage tank. *Do not seal the tank with a threaded metal top*, that is, a cap with spiral ridges that will not allow the top to blow off under extreme pressure. The air in the top of the tank will expand as it heats, building up pressure that could conceivably blow the system apart. The stopper will act as a safety valve, blowing out long before any other part can give way.

Fiberglass insulation can be wrapped around the hot-water delivery pipe to retard heat loss. The efficiency of the heater can be increased by adding foil-faced reflecting panels that will bounce more sunlight against the collector face, as indicated, *A*, Figure 25. The system can be used to provide hot water for an

Fig. 25

outside shower in your backyard or at a summer cabin (Figure 25). For areas where temperatures drop below freezing, one pint of automobile anti-freeze can be added to every five gallons of water, but remember that *anti-freeze is poison.*

Solar water heaters can also be used to space heat a doghouse (see Figure 34).

Is There a More Efficient Way to Solar-heat Water?

Yes. Conventional electric water heaters can be powered by collectors incorporating photovoltaic cells.

What Is a Photovoltaic Cell?

The solar *photovoltaic cell* is a particular kind of photocell. The best-known example of a photocell is the "electric eye" that

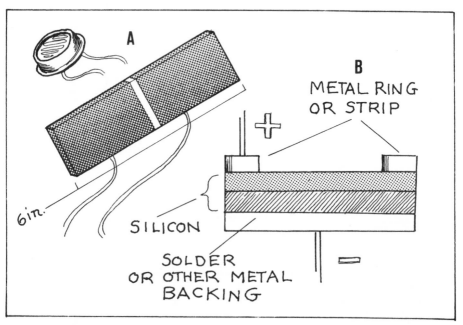

Fig. 26

opens a supermarket door when you pass in front of the cell. Certain materials—selenium and silicon in particular—generate an electric voltage when exposed to light, and this *photovoltaic effect* can be used to produce electrical power.

Figure 26 shows two typical, small photovoltaic cells, *A*. Diagram *B* shows a simplified, cross-sectional view of a typical silicon cell. The layers of an actual cell are less than 1/16″ thick. Silicon is one of the most abundant elements in the earth's crust, but to be effective as a photovoltaic agent, it must first be purified and cut with a diamond saw into very thin, wafer-like sections—a process which makes the cells very expensive. These small wafers are then assembled by the dozens, or hundreds, on a flat plate to form a solar battery that will produce direct current electricity from sunlight. About 10 percent of the solar energy falling on a given area of a cell can be converted into electricity.

As early as 1912 an electric automobile was powered by the sun striking a panel of photovoltaic cells on its roof. But it took 10,640 cells to run the car. At the present cost of silicon cells, a similar solar battery would cost roughly $40,000!

Solar collectors containing photovoltaic cells are being used to produce electricity for home use, but at rates far above those charged for conventionally produced electricity. They are practical for our adventures in outer space because they are light in weight and need no maintenance.

You can produce photovoltaic electricity to run a suitably geared model car or boat or to recharge a small battery.

PHOTOVOLTAIC BATTERY CHARGER

Figure 27 shows a photovoltaic charger. It consists of a photovoltaic cell, *A*, a small diode, *B*, and a rechargeable dry-cell battery, *C*. (A 1.5-volt battery is sufficient to power a small flashlight. Portable transistor radios are powered by two or four 1.5-volt batteries.) The cell absorbs the sun's rays and converts them into an electric current. The blocking safety diode prevents power from draining backwards from the battery. At the bottom of Figure 27 is the wiring diagram for the apparatus. The whole kit is available from the Edmond Scientific Company (see the Appendix under Suppliers).

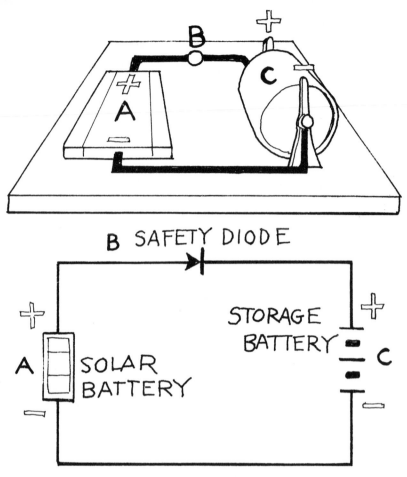

B SAFETY DIODE

A SOLAR BATTERY

STORAGE BATTERY C

Fig. 27

Are There Other Ways to Generate Electricity by Solar Power?

Yes. Solar collectors can be used to run steam engines, which turn generators to produce electricity. An early example is the eighteenth-century solar-steam engine shown in Figure 5. A number of other solar-heat engines are being developed, such as the thermoelectric converter. For more information, see *Direct Use of the Sun's Energy* under Books in the Appendix.

Most solar-steam engines and hot-air engines require a concentrating collector to provide enough heat to run them.

What Is a Concentrating Collector?

A *concentrating collector* uses reflecting surfaces to concentrate sunlight on the absorber area. The foil-covered panels used in our greenhouse (Figure 14, *B);* and with our flat-plate liquid collector, (Figure 25) qualify as concentrating collectors. Other solar devices use parabolic reflectors to concentrate the sun's rays.

What Is a Parabolic Collector?

A *parabolic collector* is a dish or bowl-shaped reflective surface with a parabolic curve. Hang a weight from a piece of string, and tie the top to a nail in a wall. If you swing the weight, it will follow a parabolic path. A parabolic curve is one whose sides are equi-distant at all points to a fixed point. A parabolic reflector can be a parabolically curved, flat surface such as that of the sun machine, Figure 5, or it can be a dish or bowl with a parabolic curve. Solar rays, striking the shiny inner surface, will be reflected to a point above its center, and can concentrate enough heat on that point to boil water or even to cook food. Such reflectors are available through the Edmond Scientific Company, listed in the Appendix. Or you can make your own solar cooker out of cardboard!

HOW TO MAKE A REFLECTING SOLAR COOKER

A solar cooker will grill hot dogs, fry bacon, eggs, and hamburgers, and make pancakes and coffee. It will also heat water for washing the dishes. All you will need are sunlight, cardboard, and patience.

To build the cooker, you must first get some corrugated pasteboard. You can recycle it from used grocery boxes, or you can buy it in large, inexpensive sheets from a moving and storage

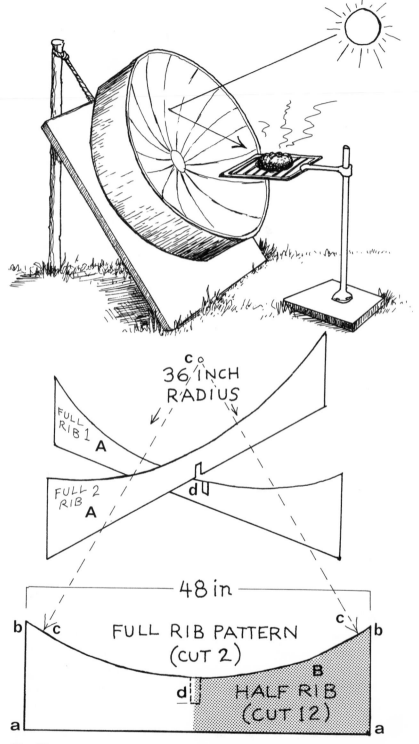

36 INCH RADIUS

c

FULL RIB 1 A

FULL 2 RIB A

d

48 in

b c FULL RIB PATTERN (CUT 2) c b

d

B
HALF RIB (CUT 12)

a a

Fig. 28

company or a box factory. Poster board, available at art supply houses, is better for the facing reflective sections, B, Figure 29, but the sections can also be made from corrugated pasteboard. You will also need:

1   roll of aluminum foil
1   small panel of ⅝" plywood
1   hamburger grill of the sort that comes with a hibachi barbecue outfit
1   roll 1½" masking tape
       rubber cement, white glue, and assorted hardware for the grill stand; hammer and saw; a sharp utility knife

Start by cutting the ribs from pasteboard, as shown in Figure 28. Take great care in laying out and cutting the cardboard pieces; the more precise your work is, the more effective the cooker will be. The two full ribs, A, are 48 inches long. The parabolic curve is that of a circle with a 36" radius. To trace the curve, first draw the base line, a-a, with its two verticals, b and b. Then use a piece of string with a pencil at its end to swing the curve from 36 inches away, as indicated, c-c.

Trace six more full ribs, and then cut them into halves at the center to make the required 12 half ribs indicated, B, Figure 28. Notch the two full ribs at the center, as shown, d. You now have two notched full ribs and 12 half ribs. Cut a square base, 48" × 48", from pasteboard. (A second base sheet, glue-laminated to the first, will make a stronger base.) Next, cut the long pasteboard strip which will form the circular side wall of the cooker, A, Figure 29. If your sheet of pasteboard is not long enough, you may have to butt two or more lengths of pasteboard together to form the whole side wall. Use your utility knife to score halfway through the side wall strip at five-inch intervals, as indicated by the dotted lines, A, in Figure 29. This will enable you to bend the wall into the required half circle, turning the scored cuts to the outside.

Now assemble the frame on its base, as shown at the top of Figure 29. First glue the circular side wall to the base. Then place the two full ribs inside the circle at right angles to one another, fitting the notches together to divide the circle into quarters.

51

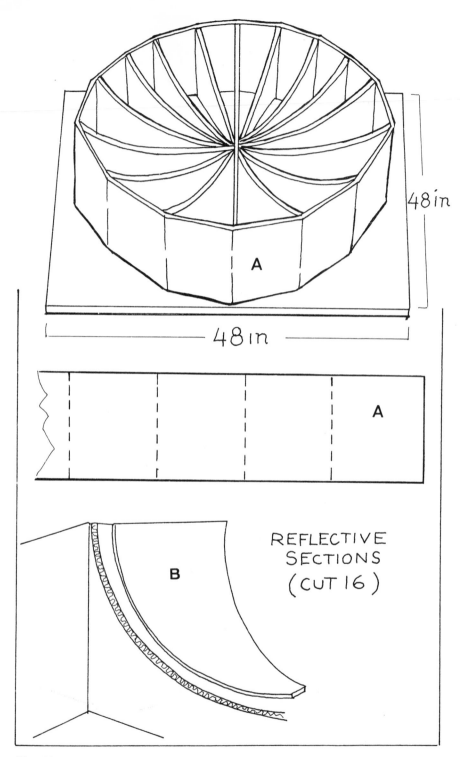

48in

48in

A

A

B

REFLECTIVE
SECTIONS
(CUT 16)

Fig. 29

Glue them into place. Glue the half ribs into place one by one, three to each quarter of the circle, spacing them equi-distant from one another.

Next, cover the concave inner surface of the cooker with 16 wedge-shaped cover sections *(B,* Figure 29). Cut these sections from pasteboard or poster board, fitting and glueing them carefully until the entire face of the cooker is covered. You will have to do some trimming as you go. To fill in the center point, cut a small circle of poster board and glue it in place to cover the juncture of all the sections.

Once you have the parabolic surface as smooth as possible, seal all the joints with strips of masking tape, running the strips over the rim and down the side wall of the cooker for a tight fit.

Now apply the aluminum foil to the parabolic surface. In order not to wrinkle the foil too badly, cut it into 16 wedge-shaped sections similar to the poster board reflector sections, *B,* Figure 29. Glue them in place with rubber cement on the cooker face, making sure the entire surface is covered with shiny foil. Finish with a final strip of masking tape placed around the entire outer rim of the cooker.

To make it easier to "aim" the cooker at the sun, you can insert a piece of stiff wire or a small curtain rod into the center of the cooker face and glue or tape it into position. It should stand straight up, about 18 inches, from the center of the parabolic surface.

Make the grill and its support from a piece of doweling or a broomstick, the barbecue grill, and assorted hardware, as shown at the top of Figure 28. It should be adjustable, with the vertical support about 40 inches long and the grill arm about 24 inches long.

The cooker itself should be propped up at an angle toward the sun, and suspended by an adjustable length of cord from a stake driven into the ground, as indicated at the top of Figure 28.

To "aim" the cooker, stand behind it and tilt it toward the sun until the shadow of the center rod disappears. This means that all of the solar rays reaching the parabolic surface will be bounced toward a four-inch area near the end of the pointer, as indicated in Figure 30. Move the grill so that its center rests exactly at that point. Pass your hand over the grill. If it feels hot, you are ready to cook.

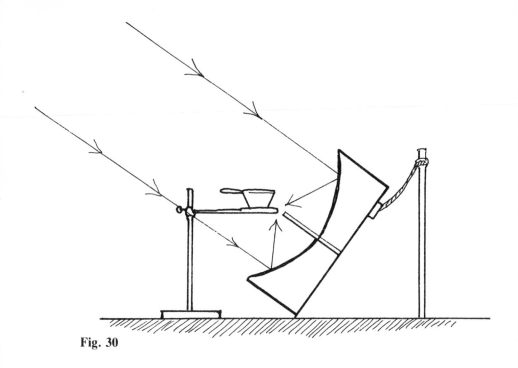

Fig. 30

Cook directly on the grill or wrap the food in foil. Grease may drip onto the reflector surface, but it can be wiped off later. You can use a small skillet for frying and a small sauce pan for heating water. Blackened pans are better, but any pan will do. Periodically adjust the reflector to track the moving sun.

It will take longer to cook this way, but you will be saving on your electric bill, which means a savings in nonrenewable fossil fuels.

What Other Uses Are There for Solar Energy?

Aside from home and water heating, solar energy has a number of special applications that are particularly useful in underdeveloped countries that do not have heavy industries or large deposits of fossil fuels and that cannot afford to buy them.

For over a century, giant solar furnaces, using parabolic reflectors and concentrating lenses, have been capable of cutting through most materials, including steel. You are creating a tiny solar furnace when you use a magnifying glass to concentrate the rays of the sun on a piece of paper, causing it to char and burn. Somewhat larger solar furnaces, built with simple tools and easily acquired materials, can be used to cut metal and other materials, solder metals, and even bake ceramics.

CONCENTRATING SOLAR FURNACE

The small furnace shown in Figure 31 is about four feet high. It can be used for melting, soldering, and baking ceramics. It

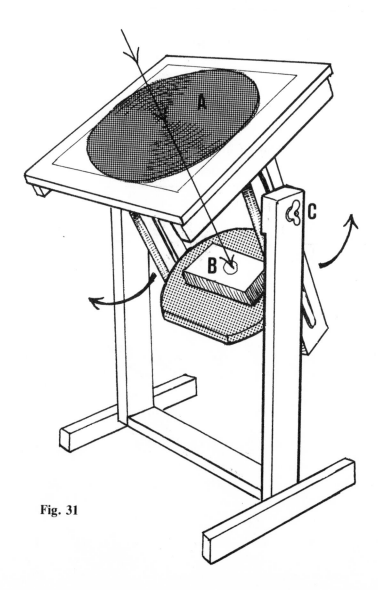

Fig. 31

uses a special, inexpensive plastic lens, called a Fresnel lens, *A*, to concentrate the rays of the sun on the center of the kiln brick, *B*. The center of the lens is kept at a right angle to the sun by tilting the table after loosening the wing nut, *C*. The wooden frame is built with common materials. Fresnel lenses are sold by some surplus stores and photographic supply dealers, and are available from the Edmond Scientific Company (see the Appendix under Suppliers. Edmond supplies complete plans along with their lens, all for the same price).

Can the Sun Be Used to Distill Fresh Water from Salt Water?

Yes, as already mentioned. Solar stills are now producing drinking water from sea water in Australia, Japan, the Greek islands, and other arid parts of the world. Similar stills can produce small amounts of water in desert areas, where even the driest earth contains some moisture. Figure 32 shows a desert

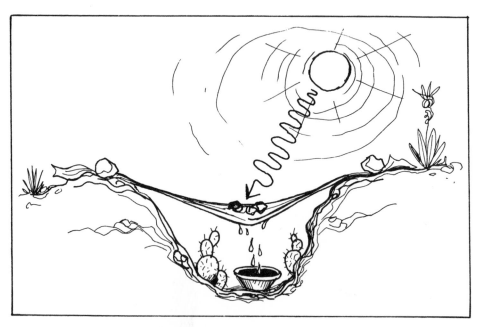

Fig. 32

survival still that requires only a sheet of transparent plastic film (to act as a cover above a depression in the earth), some rocks to hold down its edges and weight its center, and a bowl or a can to collect the water. If the still's "cover plate" is located above some growing cacti, more vapor will be produced. As night cools the air, water vapor rises from the ground. The vapor, trapped by the plastic film, drips downward into the container. All solar stills use the same drip-collection principle, including a still you can make for the distillation of fresh water from salt water.

HOW TO MAKE A SOLAR STILL

The still shown in Figure 33 consists of a panel of plywood, *A*, a glass cover panel, *B*, and two cake pans, one to hold the salt water, *C*, and a narrower pan to catch the fresh water, *D*. The second pan can be larger, as long as its edge fits under the lower

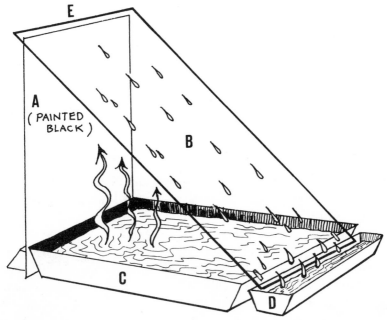

E

A
(PAINTED
BLACK)

B

C

D

Fig. 33

lip of the glass panel. ⅛", single-strength window glass will do for the cover panel.

Paint the inside of the larger pan and the inside face of the plywood panel a dull black. The upper edge of the glass cover plate, *E*, can be secured to the top edge of the plywood panel with masking tape. Put two wooden matchsticks or other small blocks of wood under the bottom edge of the glass to prop it up from the lip of the large pan. This will leave a slot through which the water, running down the inside of the cover plate, can drip freely into the collecting pan. To better contain the water vapor, add triangular panels of plywood or cardboard to either side of the still.

To operate the still, fill the large pan with salt water. Next, orient the still so that the slanting glass cover plate faces the sun. Thermal energy from the sun's rays will be trapped inside the still due to the greenhouse effect. The trapped heat will then cause the water in the larger pan to vaporize and rise to the underside of the glass panel, where it will condense into beads of water and roll down the underside of the glass into the collecting pan. Almost all of the salt will be left behind in the larger pan.

What Are the Possible Future Uses for Solar Energy?

Direct conversion of the sun's rays into energy will be providing more and more of our energy needs on a small domestic scale, in existing industry, and on vast scales barely imaginable.

In many areas of the United States, particularly south of 40° latitude, the solar heating of a well-planned solar home will pay for itself within 15 years because of lowered fuel costs. With a 25 percent drop in costs, solar heat will become cheaper than electric or oil heat in almost every part of the United States. The cost of solar hot-water systems is already low enough to make them competitive with the conventional systems in most of the country, if the investor can wait five to 15 years for the fuel savings to pay for the investment.

The performance of photovoltaic cells is being improved

through the use of concentrating lenses and new photovoltaic methods, such as the liquid-junction cell. Materials other than the expensively processed silicon are being tested, and it is possible that within ten years or so, photovoltaic cells will be inexpensive enough for use in home heating and water heating systems.

Many major corporations are working on solar systems to provide energy for agriculture, large industry, and public power. In Gila Bend, Arizona, 22,000 acres are being irrigated with pumps run by a turbine, which is powered by Freon heated by the sun. At Ohio State University, experimenters are working on a system that provides solar heat from salt ponds. A number of private and public power companies are planning vast arrays of solar collectors—some covering whole mountainsides—eventually to provide the huge amounts of power needed by industry and large urban centers. One day, rockets may carry solar collectors into space, where they will be gathered together to form huge solar-collecting "sails." The resulting power will be relayed by microwaves to receiving stations on earth.

The question is, do we want one or many of these glaring mirrors floating above our planet, visible day and night and susceptible to destruction by military means or by international vandals? Or would we do better to invest in low-tech solar systems that do not mar the environment?

Finally, test your solar knowledge by your completion of the design for a solar-heated doghouse.

Can You Build a Solar-heated Doghouse?

Figure 34 shows a way to take the chill off Rover's house during chilly nights. The suggested system combines our solar-water heating system (Figure 24) with a glass-faced heat trap on the roof and a hinged reflecting panel that can be closed at night. To work out the details, see if you can answer the following questions:

In which direction should the collecting surfaces be oriented?

Which parts of the system should be painted black?

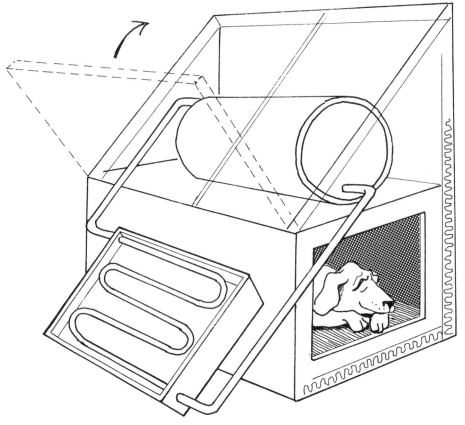

Fig. 34

Where should there be reflecting foil surfaces?

Where should there be single or double panes of glass?

Where should there be insulation?

Where should there *not* be insulation? (Keep in mind that at night the heat from the storage tank should be allowed to flow downward into the sleeping area.)

How can you safeguard against the system blowing up when the heated water and air begin to expand?

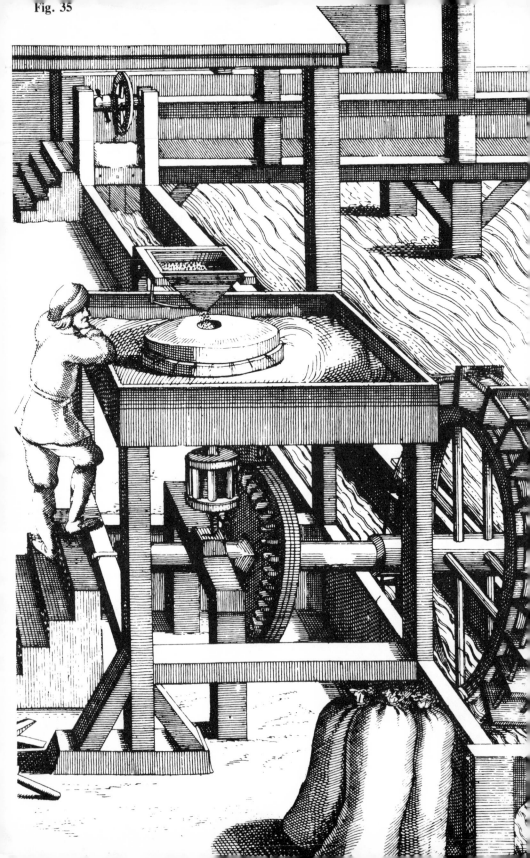

Fig. 35

3
WATER POWER

What Is Water Power?

Water power is the power of water employed to move machinery. Water, as a heavy fluid, exerts a downward pressure due to the pull of the earth's gravity. This encourages it to move, whenever it can, to a lower level. *Kinetic energy* is energy in motion, and water in motion creates the force that moves flowing streams and rivers, or causes the escape of water trapped in lakes, reservoirs, tanks, or dams. Water power can also be produced by exploitation of the oceans' tides and waves, which are caused by the gravitational pull of the moon and the sun. *Geothermal energy* is a third, separate form of water power.

How Much Water Power Is Available?

There is enough water power available in the United States to produce 84 million kilowatts of electricity a year—40 percent of our present needs. Less than half of that potential is presently developed, although there are few sites left for very large dams, which require large volumes of water between steep, narrow river banks. Russia has the potential for producing 280 million kilowatts a year, with less than 20 percent of that developed. Properly used, water power can be converted to useful work with an efficiency of from 80 to 90 percent, as compared to the 25 to 45 percent efficiencies of solar, chemical, and thermal energy systems. And water power is pollution-free.

You can persuade water power to do real work by imitating a *hydraulic,* or water machine, found in nature. Sometimes a small stone will break loose from the lip of a waterfall and become trapped in a basin in a rock bed below the falls. As the water continues to fall, it tumbles the stone around in the basin, grinding the stone smooth at the same time that it deepens the hole in which it is trapped. Such spheres of semiprecious gemstones, prized in ancient times, are still sold as "shooting marbles" in the hills of West Virginia. The sellers claim they harvest the little spheres from the gizzard of the purple mountain turkey.

HOW TO MAKE A HYDRAULIC MARBLE MACHINE

Use a hammer and a set of cold chisels (or a high-speed electric drill) to bore a hole or small pit two to four inches deep in rock located below a drop in a stream, as shown in Figure 36. The diameter of the hole depends on how large a stone you want to polish or tumble, but it should be about twice the diameter of the stone. Install a hollowed-out stem or piece of pipe (technically called a *penstock)* to better direct the flow of water into the hole. Place a partially rounded stone or a gemstone in the bottom of this grinding socket, and let time and water power do the rest.

How Old Is the Use of Water Power?

Water power is as old as the wheel. The first farmers ground grains with saddle querns like that shown in Figure 37. Next came the rotary quern, which ground grain between two circular stones mounted on a central wooden pivot. The next step was to

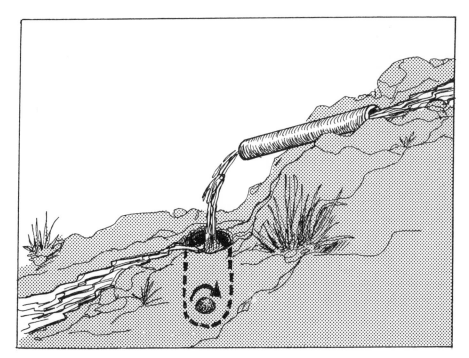

Fig. 36

Fig. 37

find an alternative energy source to turn the top, or *runner stone.* Originally, animals were used; then an early inventor noticed that stream water pushed with considerable force against any broad surface inserted at right angles to the flow. He must then have reasoned that if a series of such surfaces were attached to a wheel thrust into the water, the wheel would turn.

How Does a Waterwheel Work?

Two wheels are fitted side by side to an axle, with paddles, buckets of wood, or metal slats extending between them. The water hits the paddles, causing the wheel to turn, thus turning the axle as well. The axle is then made to turn gears, pulleys, or belts, which in turn run machinery such as a set of grindstones. The first waterwheels were probably horizontal wheels like the one shown in Figure 38. Similar wheels were in use in China as early as A.D. 31. If the wheel is set on edge, there is an increase in the kinetic energy of the falling water. The oldest surviving picture of a vertical wheel dates back to fifth-century Rome.

The three basic kinds of vertical wheels are shown in Figure 39. The overshot wheel, *A,* is located beneath the water source. The breast wheel, *B,* receives the force of the water at the

Fig. 38

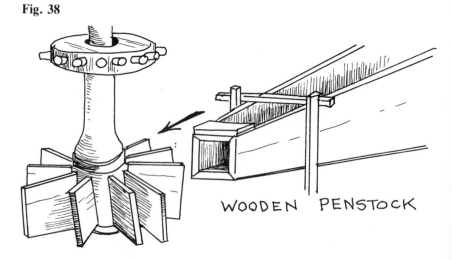

WOODEN PENSTOCK

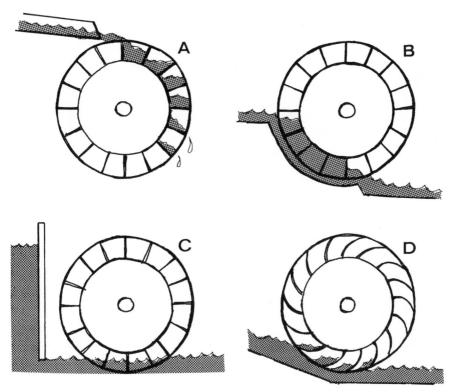

Fig. 39

midway point of its height. The undershot wheel, *C*, is moved by water pushing against the bottom of the wheel.

The most commonly used wheel, the overshot wheel, gains additional power from the gravitational weight of the water. The breast wheel is less efficient because it takes punishment from the water hitting it at midpoint. It can become jammed with floating debris. The efficiency of the undershot wheel was greatly improved in 1874 by the invention of the Poncelot wheel, *D*, Figure 39. The curved paddles, or vanes, greatly reduce the shock and turbulence of the water striking them.

How Does the Water Get to the Wheel?

The wheel can be placed directly into moving water, but usually the water is directed to the wheel by a diversion channel, flue, or penstock. Figure 40 shows how a diversion channel can turn water away from the main stream and direct it to the wheel. Figure 41 shows a dam containing a concrete or wooden flue that diverts the water and carries it to the wheel. Figure 35 (at the beginning of this chapter) shows a medieval waterwheel with a wooden flue, or sluice, to bring the water to the wheel. Water flow can be controlled by opening or closing the sluice gate, S. Water flows down the sluice and under the wheel, I, turning it and its axle, or shaft, C. Attached to this shaft is a large cogged gear called a pit wheel, which meshes with the lantern gear, E, to change the direction of the power from horizontal to vertical. The shaft of the lantern gear rises through the bran box, G, to turn the runner stone, F.

Corn, if poured into the hopper above the stones, falls through a hole in the runner stone and is caught between it and the bed stone, where it is ground. The resulting corn meal spills out between the stones into the bran box.

Tens of thousands of such waterwheels were at work around the world well past the turn of the century. They milled grain, sawed wood, turned many kinds of machinery, and even generated electricity.

Will the Stream Run Strongly Enough to Turn the Wheel?

If necessary, water can be collected and stored behind a dam, to be allowed to flow over or against the wheel when power is needed, as shown in Figures 41 and 42. The pond behind the dam contains what is called the potential of the water. The *potential* is a measure of the amount of power available in a body of water. The higher a dam is, the greater the *head*, that is, the vertical distance the water will fall when it is released. The *natural head* of a stream is the distance it drops along any given length of its natural course. The *artificial head* is any dropping distance created by artificial means, such as a dam. A dam should be located where the greatest possible head is available: on the edge of a waterfall, or where a stream is narrow, the banks high, and the current swift. Methods for calculating head-and-flow rates of water are important in any plan to build a large

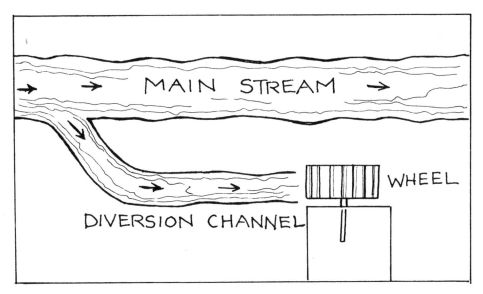

Fig. 40

Fig. 41

waterwheel. Consult books listed in the Appendix, particularly *Other Homes and Garbage.*

How Can I Use a Waterwheel to Do Work?

By building your own small, pier-mounted midstream undershot wheel.

HOW TO BUILD A WATERWHEEL ROCK TUMBLER

This wheel, Figure 44, is mounted on its own frame so that it can be moved from place to place. Because it is undershot, it can be operated in a stream as shallow as six inches deep. Its wheel can be raised or lowered within its frame. The roller mechanism is designed specifically to turn a tumbling drum for the polishing of semiprecious stones, but it can also be used to mix paint or other liquids in cans. The mechanism can be modified to do other work. Suitably geared and placed in a fast stream, it might even generate electricity. In our shallow, low-head stream, it delivers 60 rpm, that is, it turns 60 times each minute—not a bad rpm for any flat-paddle wheel.

The wheel is built from wood and metal parts available in most large hardware stores, and it can be put together with hand tools and an electric drill.

First, let's build the wheel. You will need:

1	4′ × 8′ sheet of ⅜″ plywood (exterior if available)
½	of a 4′ × 8′ sheet of ¼″ plywood (exterior if available)
1	¾″ steel axle, 25″ long
2	2″ pulley wheels with ¾″ sockets
2	4″ pulley wheels with ¾″ sockets
8	feet ½″ × ½″ wood stripping
	water-resistant glue, roofing compound, sandpaper, paint, nails, and scrap lumber.

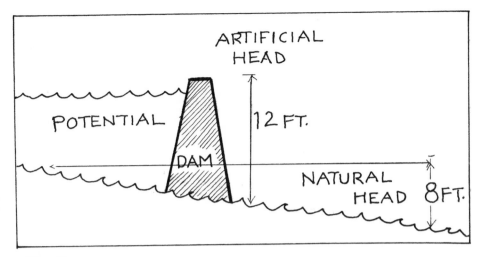

Fig. 42

Fig. 43

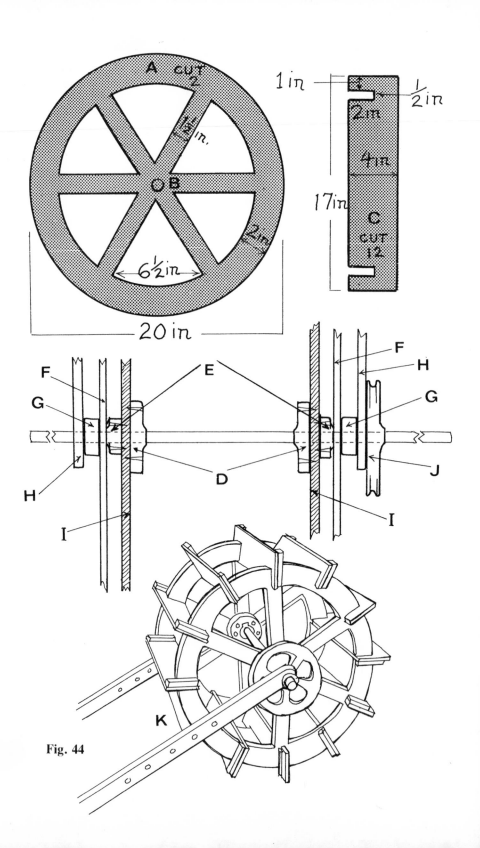

A CUT 2

1½ in.

O B

2 in

6½ in

20 in

1 in

½ in

2 in

4 in

17 in

C CUT 12

F

E

F

H

G

G

F

D

J

H

I

I

K

Fig. 44

First, cut the two-spoked wheel shapes from the ⅜″ plywood in the dimensions shown, *A*, Figure 44. Smooth all edges with a rasp or sandpaper. Drill a ⅜″ hole at the center of each, *B*, for insertion of the axle. Next, cut the 12 paddles, or vanes, from ¼″ plywood in the dimensions shown, *C*. Use wood screws to attach the wheel pulleys to the wheel shapes, fixing one 4″ pulley on the inside surface of each wheel, *D*, and one 2″ pulley on the outside, as shown, *E*. (If you wish, you can add bearings and bushings instead of the pulleys for a smoother turning axle.)

Use a pencil to mark the positions of the paddles, making sure they are equi-distant around the circle. Glue and nail the narrow ½″ strips to receive the paddles, as shown, *E*. To install the paddles, place one side of the wheel flat and prop the other above it, glueing the paddles in place, one by one, until you have the wheel completed, as shown, *K*. Allow the glue to dry, then insert the axle and tighten the set screws on each of the four pulley wheels to make sure the whole wheel holds firmly to the axle, *K*, Figure 44. Loosen the set screws again and demount the axle for reinsertion once the frame is ready.

Finally, coat the entire wheel (except for the extending lengths of axle) with asphalt roofing cement or tar, making sure to seal all cracks to prevent water from penetrating the plywood and softening the glue.

When the wheel is completed, you are ready to build the frame. You will need:

1	4′ × 8′ sheet of ⅜″ plywood (exterior if available)
3	8′ lengths of 2″ × 2″ lumber
4	3″ lengths of angle iron
2	¾″ bearings
	assorted lumber, nails, glue, roofing cement, tar, or paint

Build the frame to the dimensions shown in Figures 45 and 46, first cutting the plywood panels, *A*, *B*, *C*, then adding the framing strips of 2″ × 2″ lumber. Note the 6″ slots cut into the two panels, *A*. These will allow the wheel to be raised or lowered. Note, also, in Figure 47, that four 2″ slots, *F*, must be cut into panel *B*. These will allow adjustment of the roller mechanism later on.

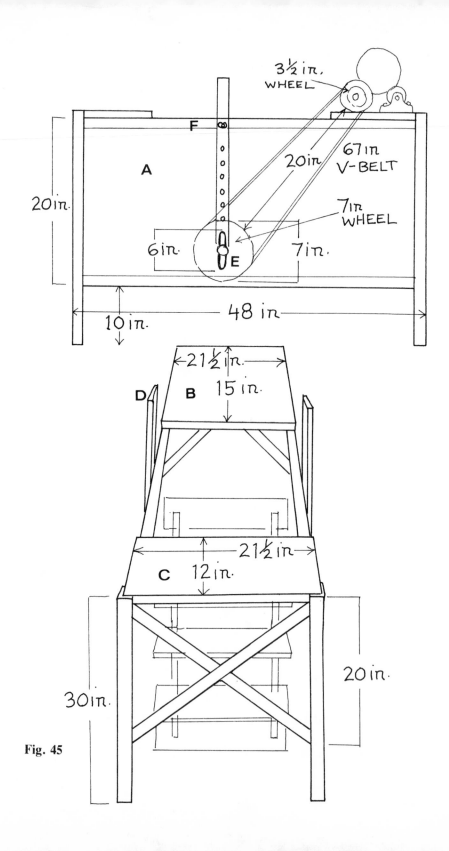

3½ in. WHEEL

F

A

20 in.

67 in V-BELT

20 in.

7 in WHEEL

6 in.

E

7 in.

48 in

10 in.

21½ in.

B   15 in.

D

C   12 in.

21½ in.

30 in.

20 in.

Fig. 45

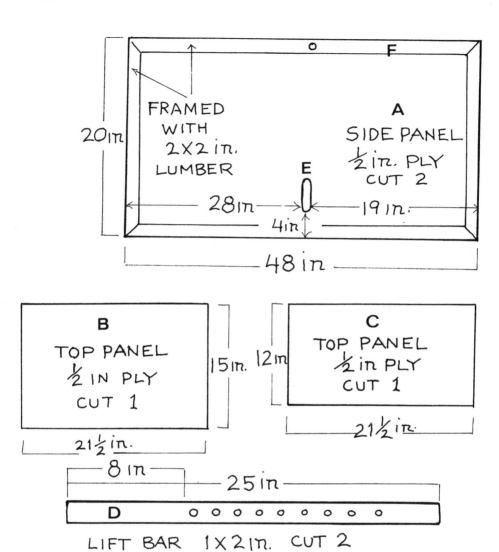

Fig. 46

Bolt an angle-iron leg to the end of each side of the frame. Before assembling, paint all parts of the frame or coat them with roofing tar. Position the two sides of the frame in their approximate positions. Then place the wheel into position between them. Slide the axle in through the holes, *E*, Figure 45, in the frame side walls, through the pulley holes in the wheel proper, and on through the opposite side of the wheel and the frame. Temporarily tack on the top cross panels, *B* and *C*, and the X-braces at either end. Turn the wheel, taking great care that the whole frame is square to allow the wheel to turn freely without scraping the sides. You must have at least a ¾" clearance for the wheel at all points. When you are sure all is well, glue and nail the frame permanently together, with the wheel correctly seated inside and the axle ends extending from either side of the frame. Finally, add the lifting mechanism. This consists of two vertical pieces of 1" × 3" lumber (D, Figure 46) drilled with spaced holes and with axle sockets at their ends. Bearings can be inserted to allow the axle to turn more easily. Note the 1" wooden washers placed, G, Figure 45, to hold, or shim, the lift bars out from the frame. The vertical lift bars are secured by bolts and wing nuts, as shown, F, Figure 45. The lifts should always be positioned at equal heights on each side in order to hold the wheel level inside the frame.

With the frame completed and the wheel installed, you are now ready to add the rock-tumbling mechanism. You will need:

1	7" pulley wheel with a ¾" socket
1	3½" pulley wheel with a ½" socket
1	67" fan or pulley belt to fit the wheels
2	15" rollers with bearings and mounts
1	rock-tumbling drum approximately 7" × 10"

Assemble the tumbling mechanism as shown in Figure 47. We used rubber rollers, recycled from an old IBM copying machine found at a junk store. Old washing machine or typewriter rollers will do, or you can fabricate your own from lengths of 2" stair railing run through with ½" steel axles. Another alternative is to use rollers made from 3" plastic pipe with wooden inserts and steel axles. The surfaces of these rollers can be rubberized by slipping on sleeves cut from bicycle inner tubes. If you search surplus stores and junk yards, you may find the parts you need.

The rollers should be mounted on bearings. Bearings can be purchased with their own mounts, as shown in Figure 47, or bearings with ½" sockets can be purchased and mounted in routed wooden blocks. Note that our mountings are secured to the panel by bolts inserted through the 2" slots, F. The bolts have wing nuts underneath the panel which allow the rollers to be moved forward and back to tighten or loosen the pulley belt.

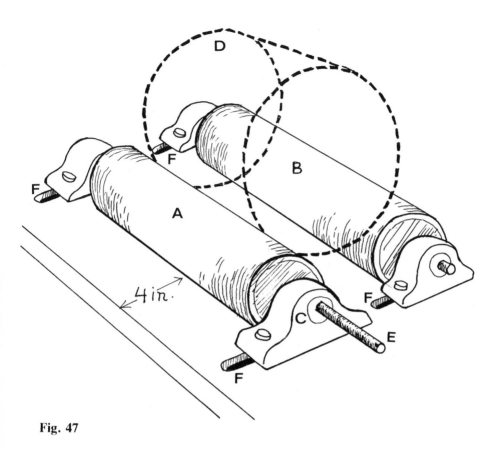

Fig. 47

Once the rollers are in place, install the belt, and you will have a direct power drive from the turning wheel to the tumbling mechanism.

The rock-tumbler drum can be made from a 10″ length of iron water pipe. We used pipe with a ¼″ thick wall, plugged at both ends with wooden discs. The tumbling drum must be watertight. Professional drums are lined inside with rubber for longer life, and can be purchased from one of the many suppliers who advertise in the lapidary magazines listed in the Appendix. For instructions on the use of tumbling drums and the various mixtures of grit required to polish stones, see *Pebble Collecting and Polishing,* listed in the Appendix under Books.

How Is Electricity Made from Water Power?

Most effectively, by damming a flow of water to gain sufficient power potential and head to drive some form of *water turbine*, which in turn runs a generator that produces electricity.

What Is a Turbine?

An enclosed waterwheel. In 1827 a French engineer named Fourneyron designed a steel wheel housed inside a steel drum. It let water in through a ring of fixed blades that were curved in the opposite direction to the vanes of the running wheel. This caused a calculated turbulence within the enclosure and produced much more power than an open wheel. There are two main classes of turbines: the *reaction turbine* and the *impulse turbine*. Giant versions of both are used in combination with huge dams to produce large amounts of hydroelectrical power.

Are There Turbines for Small-scale Production of Electricity?

Yes. The Pelton wheel, shown in Figure 48, has specially shaped bucket cups. Water is delivered from the source in a closed pipe or penstock, *A*, and directed against the cups by a nozzle, *B*, striking the wheel in alternating bursts or jets, thus classifying it as an impulse turbine. Pelton wheels can be as small as a shoebox or as large as a barrel. The wheel turns a *generator*, or *alternator*, which produces an electric current. The power can be used directly or stored in batteries for later use. The generator usually produces *direct current* (DC) electricity, but DC can be changed to household *alternating current*, or AC, by the use of a device called an *inverter*. (See Chapter Four, Wind Power.) Furthermore, a Pelton wheel requires a head or fall of water of at least 50 feet. This means an impossibly high dam for most home construction, so the production of electricity by small turbines is presently economical only in mountain areas where streams produce natural heads of from 50 to 200 feet as they tumble

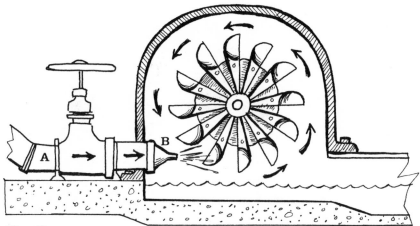

Fig. 48

down mountainsides. Many such wheels are producing household electricity in isolated homesteads in the Rocky Mountain states.

    The best of the small turbines, however, can supply only a portion of the enormous electrical needs of the average American household, so its use must be coupled with conservation. (See Chapters Four and Six for household energy needs.)

How Can I Test the Effectiveness of the Pelton Wheel?

    Test the Pelton wheel by making an experimental model powered by your kitchen faucet.

HOW TO MAKE AN EXPERIMENTAL PELTON WHEEL

    As shown in Figure 49, the wheel consists of a wooden disc with cupped buckets turning on an axle. Cut a 20″ wheel from a

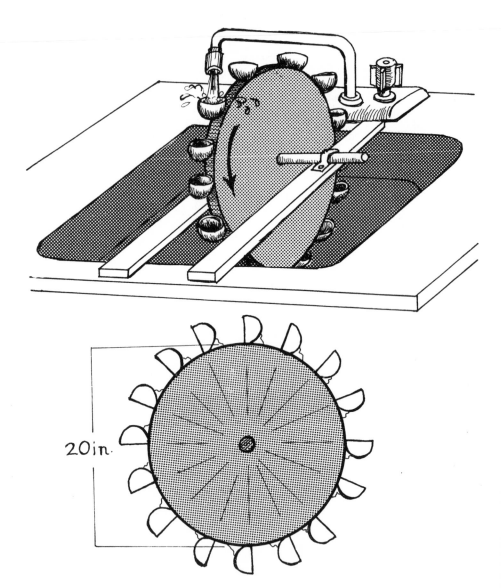

20 in.

Fig. 49

piece of 1″ plywood. (If your sink is too small, make a smaller wheel with fewer buckets.) Make the buckets from Ping-Pong balls cut in half. Fasten the balls to the rim of the wheel, spacing them evenly and glueing with epoxy glue. Bore a ⅛″ hole through the center of the disc and insert a ¼″ steel rod as an axle, making sure you have a tight enough fit to turn the wheel. Mount the wheel on a wooden frame like the one shown in Figure 49, and position it beneath a water faucet. By experimentally turning the faucet on and off, you can imitate the spurting jets of water that make an impulse turbine turn.

The wheel can be any size you wish. The axle might be rigged to do light work with a pulley system similar to that used on the waterwheel in Figure 43. With some experimentation, you might rig it up to turn a small bicycle generator and produce small amounts of electricity, as with our bicycle wind generator in Chapter Four.

How Does the Ocean Produce Power?

The ocean contains two potential sources of power: waves and tides. The tides are caused by the gravitational pull of the sun and moon on the earth, causing oceans to bulge and shift in their basins. Waves are the result of this shifting, which is similar to the way water sloshes in a tilted bowl.

The most obvious method of using tidal energy is to insert an undershot wheel into the water and let the outgoing tide turn it. Before the advent of cheap electricity, many such tidal wheels powered mills all over the world. They were usually located in bays or inlets where they were protected from storms and heavy waves. One such installation sits astride the River Rance in Brittany, France, close to the place where the river joins the sea. This tidal energy plant produces enough electricity to power a small city.

A number of ingenious devices have been suggested for using the force of traveling ocean waves to produce useable power. One such wave machine is called the "Sea Horse," A, Figure 50. It uses the action of waves to alternately raise and lower floating cylinders (producing an effect much like that of cylinders operating in an automobile engine), turning a crank-

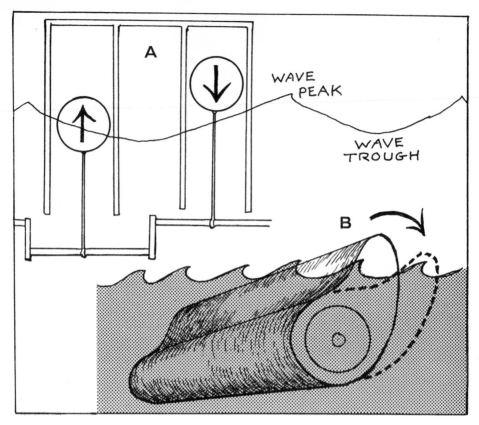

Fig. 50

shaft that could turn a generator. Another wave machine, *B*, uses cam-shaped floats to produce power. The floats, each about five feet long, are connected as one long string of floats, arranged to face oncoming waves. As a wave strikes each float, it rocks back to let the wave flow over. This creates suction within the mechanism to operate hydraulic pumps, which, in turn, are used to power generators. Thus, bobbing like ducks before the push of each wave, the floats produce electricity.

A final, separate use of water power is the exploitation of *geothermal energy.*

What Is Geothermal Energy?

The core of the earth is molten and tremendously hot,

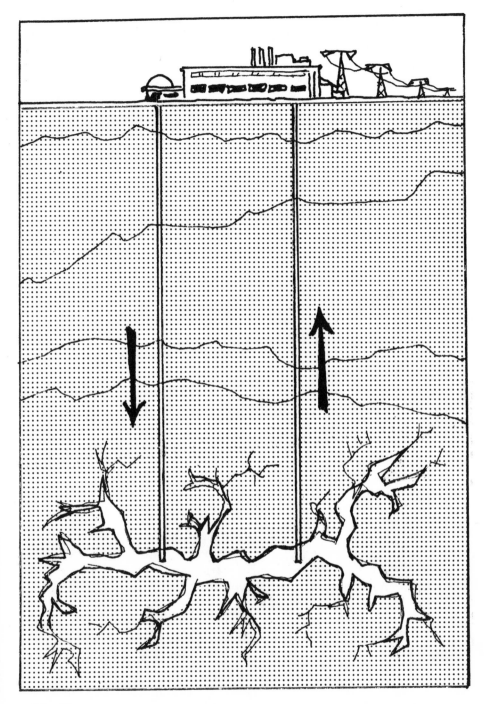

Fig. 51

heating portions of the earth's mantle, or crust, closer to the surface. When subterranean water comes into contact with hot rock, it turns to steam, and sometimes boils up through cracks in the rock and out of vents at the rock's surface. "Old Faithful," the well-known geyser in Yellowstone Park, is an example of a thermal spout. Such natural formations can be used to run steam engines, which turn generators to produce electricity. A geothermal plant in Larderello, Italy, generates nearly 400,000 kilowatts of electricity. The United States has only a limited number of natural geothermal formations, located mainly in Alaska, Wyoming, Montana, and California. The only geothermal plant presently operating in the United States is located in California's Sonoma Valley. It has a generating capacity equal to the Larderello facility.

Scientists believe that it is possible to dig deep wells wherever there is hot rock within 25,000 feet of the earth's surface, and to force cold water into the wells, where it would be heated. The resulting steam could be used to run steam turbines for the production of electricity (see Figure 51). However, there is a risk that this underground thermosiphoning might touch off earthquakes and even cause a serious collapse in the earth's surface.

What Are the Possible Future Uses of Water Power?

Governments and private industries will continue to build large dams and giant turbines for the production of vast amounts of electricity, particularly where the best hydroelectric sites have not yet been exploited, as in Africa and South America. But there must be a limit to this exploitation since the interruption of major rivers and streams tends to change the landscape, reduce the spawning of fishes, and otherwise jolt the ecological balance.

Since the energy crisis and the movement of many young Americans back to small parcels of land, there has been a slow but steady increase in the use of low-tech water power systems.

Among these are old-fashioned wooden wheels for mechanical work and small turbines for the generation of limited amounts of domestic electricity. The development and spread of this kind of low-tech equipment will be particularly vital to the economies of underdeveloped countries without fossil fuel resources.

Certain of the schemes for harnessing tidal and wave power will eventually prove practical, but there is a serious question as to whether the energy gains will justify the existence of ten-mile-long, coastal wave machines that could tangle navigation, possibly break up in storms, and deposit more debris on our beaches.

4

WIND POWER

What Is Wind Power?

Wind power is the potential of kinetic energy to move air. The winds are the result of the earth's daily revolution under the rays of the sun. Sunlight heats the surface of the earth and causes bodies of air to expand (see Figure 6). But this process is not evenly distributed over the landscape. In some places, because of clouds or valleys, the rising air is cooler at sundown than it is in other areas. The bodies of sun-heated air seek out these cooler bodies of air and rush into them. This rushing movement in the air gases is what we call wind.

How Is Wind Power Put to Work?

By interposing a flat surface at an angle across the air flow. Anybody who has tried to manoeuver a piece of plywood across open ground on a windy day knows how powerful the wind can be. For thousands of years this force has been used to propel sailing ships.

A square-rigger can run downwind with its sails at exact right angles to the wind flow. That is possible because the hull skids through a low-resistance element: water. If the ship was fixed to the earth, a high and gusty wind would most likely tear

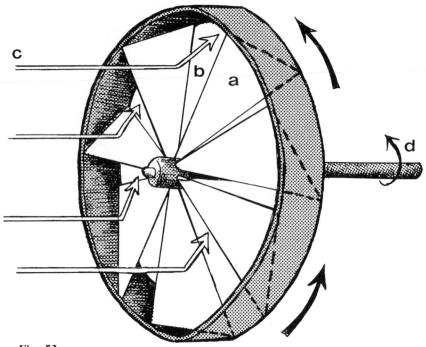

Fig. 53

away the masts. This is one reason why the *sails,* or *vanes,* of the basic wind wheel shown in Figure 53 have spaces between them. Part of the wind flow, *c,* will strike the vanes a glancing blow, *b,* while the other part will be allowed to pass through. This filtering effect prevents the wind from tearing the wheel from its tower. The glancing, angled force of the wind pushes the vanes, *a,* partly sideways, causing the wheel to turn and its axle to develop *torque, d,* or the twisting motion that can be harnessed by means of a pulley, geared wheel, or crankshaft.

How Much Wind Power Is Available?

Fifty-seven percent of the energy available in the wind at any particular place can be captured by the best of wind machines. Only 70 percent of that captured energy can be used to pump water or do other mechanical work. And only 30 percent of the captured energy can be transformed by a wind generator into electricity. There are formulas for measuring the kinetic energy available in a given mass of moving air (see *Other Homes and Garbage*, listed in the Appendix).

For our limited purposes, the most useful measurement of wind power is its *velocity:* how fast it moves in miles per hour (mph). Most traditional windmills require a 10 mph wind to get started. Electricity-producing wind generators require averages of from 10 to 25 mph.

Can I Measure the Wind's Velocity?

You can get a very rough estimate by observing the physical effects of the wind (Figure 54). At less than 1 mph, one, the air is

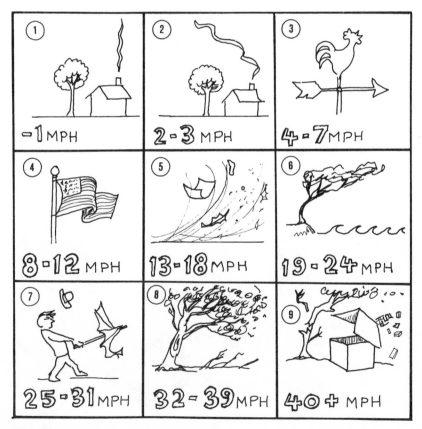

Fig. 54

calm and smoke will rise straight up. At from 2 to 3 mph, two, smoke drifts, but a common weather vane will not yet swing around to show wind direction. Between 4 and 7 mph, three, the weather vane shows wind direction, the leaves on the trees begin to rustle, and you can feel the wind on your face. Between 8 and 12 mph, four, leaves and twigs are in constant motion and a lightweight flag will extend out from its pole. Between 13 and 18 mph, five, the wind will raise dust and loose paper, and small branches of trees will move. Between 19 and 24 mph, six, small trees begin to sway and small waves form on inland waters. Between 25 and 31 mph, seven, large tree branches are set in motion, umbrellas can fly away, and telephone wires whistle. Between 32 and 39 mph, eight, whole trees sway, and people have to lean slightly forward as they walk upwind.

For a more accurate measurement of wind velocity, you can make your own hand-held wind gauge.

HOW TO MAKE A CALIBRATED WIND GAUGE

This do-it-yourself wind gauge, Figure 55, can be used to arrive at a rough estimate of wind speed. Similar, inexpensive gauges are available from the Edmond Scientific Company, and other Suppliers listed in the Appendix. To make the gauge, you will need:

1	plastic or metal protractor
1	Ping-Pong ball
1	30 centimeter length of monofilament nylon fishing line, about 0.08 mm in diameter
1	small spirit level
1	wooden or metal handle

A spirit level is a short length of closed glass tube containing oil or water and a bubble of air. By aligning the level with any

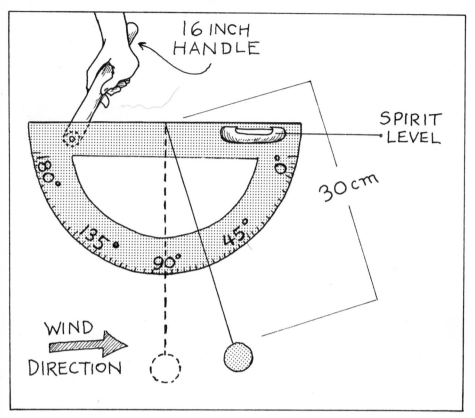

Fig. 55

surface so that the air bubble locates at the center of the tube, you can adjust the surface to be exactly parallel to sea level.

The spirit level is not absolutely necessary, but if you have one, cement it to the protractor as shown. Attach the nylon line to the Ping-Pong ball and suspend it from the center of the protractor, as shown. Attach a handle which will enable you to hold the device at right angles to the wind flow and away from your body so as to minimize air disturbance. Make sure the flat edge of the protractor is level. The wind will push at the Ping-Pong ball, causing the nylon line to swing. Determine the angle of swing from the protractor's markings. For instance, if the wind holds the nylon filament out to about 60°, as shown, check the calibration chart, and you will arrive at a wind speed of 14.9 mph.

91

Calibration Data

Angle	mph
90°	0
85°	5.8
80°	8.2
75°	10.1
70°	11.8
65°	13.4
60°	14.9
55°	16.3
50°	18.1
45°	19.6
40°	21.4
35°	23.4
30°	25.5
25°	28.7
20°	32.5

Regular, periodic measurements (every hour) can be totalled over a period of 24 hours and then divided by the number of measurements to give you the average daily wind speed.

How Old Is the Use of Wind Power?

Wind power was probably first used by a caveman astride a floating log, spreading his fur garment to catch the wind. Primitive windmills were in use in Persia during the tenth century A.D., and there is inconclusive evidence that they appeared 300 years earlier. The first written record of a typical European windmill, with vertically oriented sails, dates from A.D. 1185, in England. By the end of the fourteenth century, the windmill was common in most of Europe.

How Did the Early Windmills Work?

Figure 56 shows a typical sixteenth-century post mill. It had

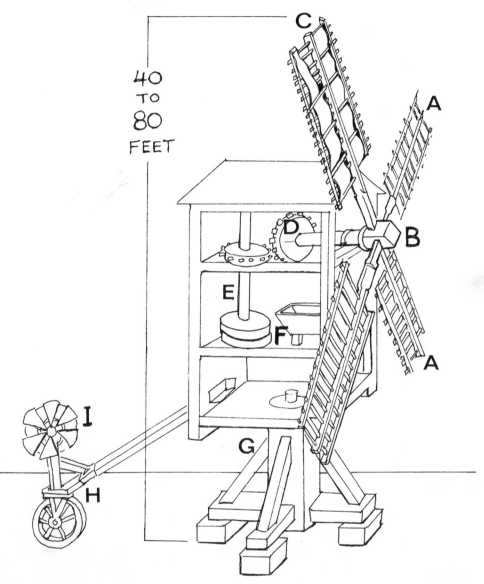

C

40
TO
80
FEET

A

D

B

E

F

I

G

H

A

Fig. 56

its entire mechanism enclosed in a roofed box. It was mounted on a huge swivel post and set into an open trestle on the ground, *G.* The wind wheel was composed of sails attached to long tapering wooden spars, called stocks, *A.* They crossed at right angles and were mortised to a hub on the end of the horizontal wind shaft, *B.* Strips of canvas, *C,* were laced through the latticework sail bars attached to each stock. At the inside end of the horizontal shaft, *B,* was a large, geared wheel, *D,* called the brake wheel, because it had wooden brake shoes for stopping the mill (they often failed). The brake wheel meshed with gears at the top of the vertical main post, *E.* The main post then turned grinding stones or other machinery below it, *F.*

A windmill must always keep its sails turned toward the wind. Otherwise, the wind might pass behind the sails and tear them loose. For this reason, the housing of a mill was allowed to swivel on its post and trestle, *G.* At first, the entire housing was turned by hand. The miller grasped the tail post, *H,* and slowly walked the mill around to face the wind. This heavy work was eased by the addition of wheel trucks at the end of the post, and eventually by the addition of a small wind wheel, *I.* As the wind shifted, it caused this vaned wheel to turn and, by a system of gears, to slowly truck the mill around to once again face into the wind.

The traditional windmill turned too slowly to power the new machinery made possible by the development of better iron and steel. By the early nineteenth century, it began to be replaced by the *annular* wind wheel, which consisted of a circle of vanes arranged radially, as in Figure 57. The individual vanes on these wheels, or *rotors,* were made of metal, and were tipped at an angle to the wind, resulting in the steel water-pumping windmill. Hundreds of thousands of these windmills have been used to extract subsoil water and to open formerly useless land to agriculture, particularly on the great plains of the American frontier. They are still operating wherever cheap electricity is not available for water pumping: Australia, South America, and Africa. We have used such an annular rotor for our bicycle-wheel, electric-wind plant, Figure 59, because it is much easier to construct than the propeller that replaced it on modern wind generators.

Fig. 57

How Is Electricity Generated from Wind Power?

By using a propeller to turn a generator. The generator produces electricity which is stored in batteries. Figure 58 shows the layout of a modern wind-generating plant. The generator, *A*, converts the mechanical energy produced by the propeller shaft into direct current electricity. (A machine called an *alternator* can produce the alternating current used in most homes, and for special reasons, some wind plants use an alternator with a rectifier, but the result is the same: DC current.)

The *voltage regulator*, *B*, absorbs the alternating weak and strong surges caused by varying wind speeds and adjusts the

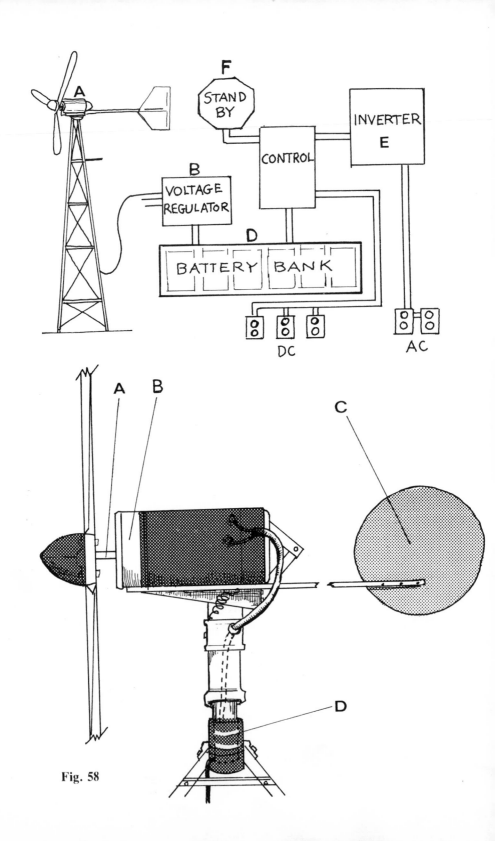

Fig. 58

output of the generator so that it always supplies the proper voltage to the batteries. *(Voltage* is a measure of what might be called the "volume" of electrical current. For a complete explanation of volts, amps, and watts, consult *Other Homes and Garbage,* Appendix.) *Batteries, D,* store energy for use when the wind is not strong enough for the generator to produce a usable current. The batteries take in and send out DC only.

The *inverter, E,* converts the DC current to AC. Originally, most electricity was transmitted as direct current, but most modern appliances operate more efficiently on alternating current, so most modern home systems are entirely AC. Since some appliances can use DC directly from the battery bank and some cannot, the system shown sends some DC directly to DC outlets in the house and some through the inverter to AC outlets. This requires both kinds of outlets in the house, but since the inverter is very expensive, and also uses up power, dividing the distribution of power is often an economical solution.

Because the usual bank of batteries cannot store enough power for more than three or four days, a standby system, *F,* is often necessary. This usually consists of a small gasoline motor and an alternator producing AC.

The bottom diagram (Figure 58) shows the wind generator itself. An airplane propeller is not suitable because it is designed to move air, not be moved by it. The wind generator propeller has blades with a cross section resembling an airplane wing. A three-bladed propeller, or rotor, is more stable than a two-bladed one. When the wind blows, the rotor turns the shaft, *A,* which enters the gear housing, *B,* where gears increase the turning speed to meet the higher rpm needs of the generator. Although the generator is heavy, it is usually mounted on the top of the tower and in line with the rotor shaft. The reason for this is because the wind plant must be allowed to swivel atop its tower in order to always face the wind. Transforming the power of the turning shaft from horizontal to vertical requires more gears that would absorb too much of the torque. The rotor and its generator are made to swivel by the tail vane, *C.* A simple length of wire could be used to carry the current down the tower to the ground, except for the fact that the generator turns around and around and would eventually twist the wire around the tower and break it. This problem is solved by a device called a *slip ring assembly, D,* which transfers the current while still allowing the wind plant to turn freely above. The current is then conducted through the voltage regulator to the batteries for storage.

How Can You Generate Electricity from Wind Power?

By building one of the two wind generators described below.

HOW TO BUILD A BICYCLE-WHEEL WIND PLANT

In a 15 to 20 mph wind, this wind plant can generate enough electricity to light a bicycle head lamp, which can be used as a porch light, *A*, Figure 59. To build it, you will need:

1	old bicycle. You need only the front wheel, complete with tire and good bearings, and the frame, complete with front fork. A 28″ wheel is best, but 26″ will do. Old bikes can be picked up at country auctions or junk stores for very reasonable prices.
1	bicycle generator of the type that operates on friction from the turning tire. The better units cost a few dollars more, but the difference in efficiency is worth the extra expense.
1	bicycle headlamp, usually sold with the generator
15	square feet of Alclad or other do-it-yourself aluminum sheeting. The light aluminum used for roof flashing is adequate.
1	4′ length of ½″ copper tubing
	assorted minor hardware, common hand tools, paint

First, disassemble the bicycle by removing the handlebars, front wheel, rear wheel and sprocket, and front sprocket and

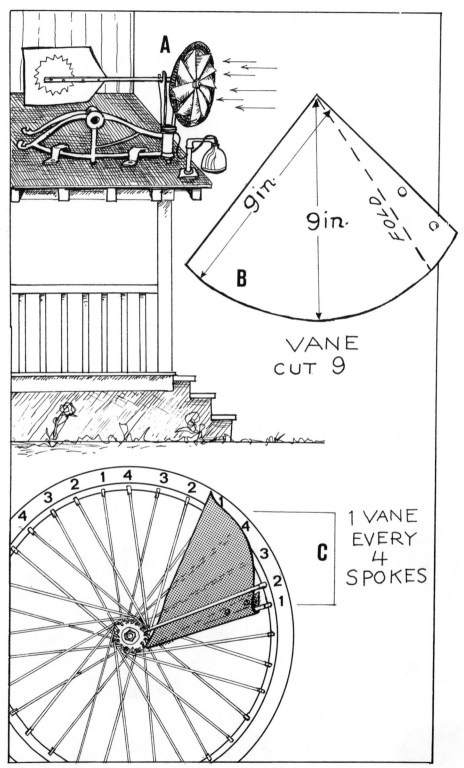

A

B 9in. 9in. FOLD

VANE
CUT 9

C 1 VANE
EVERY
4
SPOKES

Fig. 59

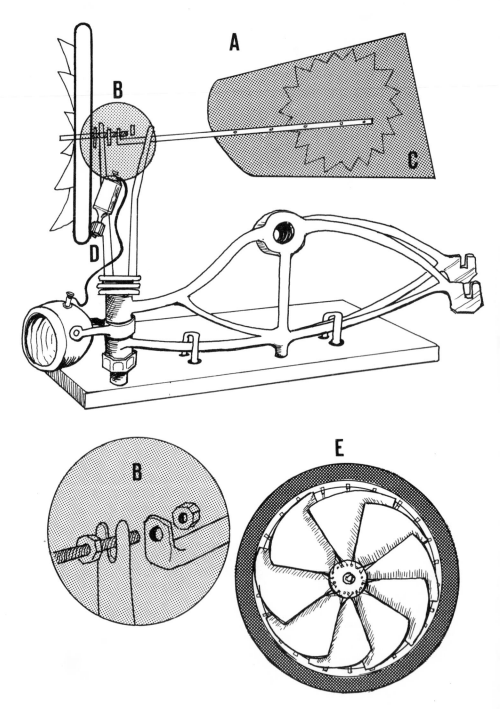

Fig. 60

pedal assembly. The pedal assembly can be removed by first removing the footpiece, then the lock washers and bearings, and finally the angled crankshaft.

Next, convert the front wheel into an annular wind wheel by adding aluminum vanes, as indicated in Figure 59. Cut the nine vanes from sheet aluminum in the shape and dimensions shown, *B*. These vanes are for a 26″ wheel. A 28″ wheel will take slightly larger vanes. Fold each vane on the dotted line. Insert each vane so that it folds over one spoke and under the next, as indicated, *C*. Crimp the fold tight to the first spoke with pliers, or secure it with small bolts or rivets. Repeat the process every four spokes. Each vane should slightly overlap the one preceding it until all nine are in place and the wheel looks like the illustration *(E,* Figure 60). Take the wheel outdoors and hold it by the axle ends, facing it into the wind. Efficiency can be improved by bending the outside ends of the vanes slightly upward to form a concaved scoop effect. Clean and regrease the axle and bearings so that the wheel turns easily on its shaft. Make sure the tire is fully inflated and will not leak or deflate.

Next, invert the bicycle frame, grasp the ends of the fork, and spread them about two inches, taking care not to exert so much pressure that you break the welds. You will need about a six-inch gap between the two ends of the fork. Position the vaned wheel so that its front surface faces away from the open end of the fork. Mount it, as shown, (Figure 60*B*) and secure it with both bolts to the single forward tine of the fork. Clean and grease the bearings where the fork meets the frame so that the fork will move easily and allow the wheel to track around to face the wind.

Now you are ready to add the rear vane which will cause the wheel to always face the wind. First, flatten one end of the copper tubing. Then drill a ¼″ hole and bend the flattened end at right angles, as shown, insert *B*, Figure 60. Cut the rear vane, *C*, from sheet aluminum, then attach it to the length of tubing with bolts or rivets in the position shown, *A*. Make sure it is vertical to the ground and to the bend in the opposite end of the tube. Crimp the tube about five inches back from its bent end so that the crimp rests in the notch at the end of the rear tine of the fork, insert *B*. Secure the bent end against the wheel shaft, as shown in *B*, adding a third nut to hold it to the shaft. Finally, hammer the

101

tubing at the crimp point so that it fits into the notch in the rear fork tine. If it does not fit securely, wrap it in place with wire or tape, or solder it.

Install the generator as it would be installed on a bicycle, as shown, *D*. The friction wheel should be pressed against the side of the wheel. Attach the wire that leads to the lamp to its proper pole, then lead it down to the lamp. Make sure that the lamp is also grounded to a rod thrust in earth.

You may now mount the inverted bicycle frame atop a small tower or porch roof. Try to choose a position open to prevailing winds and not interrupted by walls or trees. Some adjustment of the generator position may be necessary. It should press against the tire with enough pressure to turn it, but not hard enough to stop the wheel. As your wind plant turns to meet the wind, the wire may eventually become wrapped around the fork. You must then unhook it before it breaks. The solving of this problem with a slip ring assembly is unfortunately too technical for this book, but you will find that the winds usually prevail from one direction and the plant seldom swings around a full 360° circle.

Fig. 61

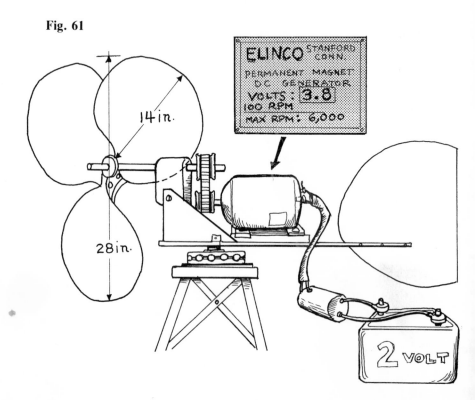

Figure 61 suggests a more efficient wind plant which generates about the same wattage, but can be hooked up to store the electricity generated. The unit shown uses a 14″ ventilation fan as a rotor, coupled to a small generator by a belt-and-gear system purchased at a junk shop. A suitable voltage regulator regulates the power surge between wind plant and battery. But, the small 3.9-volt generator shown is hard to come by, because it is available only at a few electrical supply outlets. For this reason, we have not included detailed plans here. However, with the help of a trained adult, you can put together your own version from junk shop parts, perhaps using a six-volt alternator from a 1960-or-earlier model Volkswagen. The two-volt battery shown in Figure 61 is a cheap bulky unit sometimes sold by the telephone company.

Can Wind Power Generate Enough Electricity for a Home?

In 1915 there were 3,000 windmills producing electricity for homes in Denmark. Wind generators supplied electricity for thousands of isolated farms and homesteads across the United States in the 1930s and 1940s, until the government's rural electrification program began to provide cheap electricity from the giant fossil-fuel power plants.

But those early farmers and homesteaders got by on much less electricity than we do (see Chapter Six). Today, the average American home gobbles up at least 400 kilowatt hours (kwh) per month; many consume 550 kwh and more. The best modern wind generator available for home use (Elektra of Switzerland) has a rated output of 6,000 watts. This means that with a yearly average wind speed of 10 mph, it can produce a monthly output of only 400 kwh. And it costs over $10,000 to install, complete with shutdown system, tower, power lines, storage batteries, and backup system.

At present, the average large community power plant delivers electricity for only a few cents per kwh. Even if the cost of a private wind system is written off over the years, the electricity it produces still costs about seven times as much as public power.

103

But all is not lost. First of all, home electricity consumption can be reduced by giving up luxuries such as air conditioners and color television sets (see Chapter Six). Furthermore, the integrated approach to home energy systems, also discussed in Chapter Six, can use other alternative sources of power to reduce the need for wind-generated electricity to within easy reach of the Elektra or an even smaller machine. Moreover, the cost of electricity has been going steadily up and will probably continue to do so. Finally, wind power is actually cheaper than conventional power in terms of depletion of the fossil fuels and damage to the environment.

Is There an Alternative to the High-speed Wind Plant?

Yes. The *Savonius,* or *S-rotor,* windmill was invented about 45 years ago. It consists of two half drums mounted on a vertical axle, as shown in Figure 62. The wind strikes the cupped inside surface of one face, curls around to strike the opposite face, and then pushes it around to catch more wind. Because one-half of its driving surface is always facing the wind, there is no need for a

Fig. 62

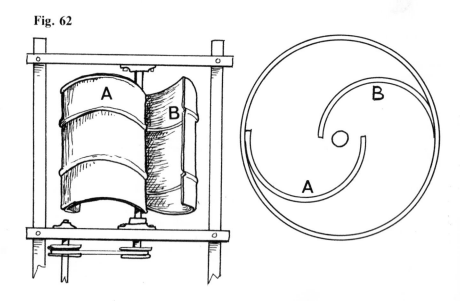

tail vane to push it around. Another advantage is the vertical axle, which carries the rotational force directly to the ground. Thus, a heavy generator need not be balanced on top, but can be located at the base of the tower.

The main disadvantage of the Savonius is that it is much slower than the two- or three-bladed propeller and less than half as efficient at converting the wind's energy. It must be large to make up for its inefficiency, but the larger it is, the less stable it is.

However, it is easily fabricated by the home craftsman from converted 55-gallon oil drums. A number of these homemade machines are presently providing a minimum of electricity for isolated farms and homesteads. You can make a working model of a Savonius windmill.

HOW TO MAKE A SAVONIUS ROTOR FISH-POND AGITATOR

Figure 63 suggests a Savonius windmill for the agitation and aeration of water in a fish tank or small pond.

To make the model you will need:

1   no. 30 metal can, the sort that is used as a container for bulk canned goods, or any drum-shaped container. (You can even make the model from a Quaker Oats container.)

1   30" length of ¼" iron rod (Or an equivalent length of wooden doweling, if you are using the Quaker Oats drum.)

1   18" × 10" piece of galvanized iron (Or an equivalent sheet of poster board, if using the cardboard drum.)

1   1" spiraled wood drill
     solder, soldering equipment, assorted hardware and tools. (Also glue, if using the wood and cardboard drum.)

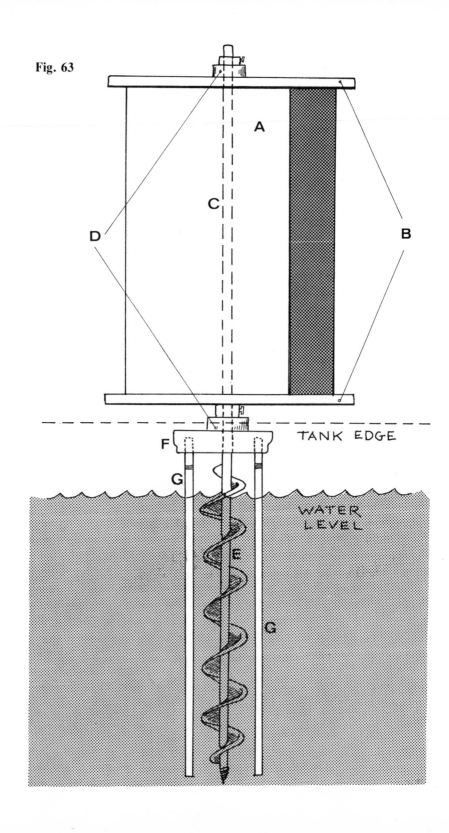

Fig. 63

A

B

C

D

TANK EDGE

F

G

E

WATER
LEVEL

G

Figure 63 diagrams the general construction. The first step is to use a hacksaw, coping saw, saber saw, or emery wheel to cut the drum lengthwise into equal halves. The drum assembly, *A*, consists of two round discs, *B*, with the two drum halves positioned between them in the configuration shown in Figure 62, *A* and *B*. Cut the discs from sheet metal (or from poster board, if using a cardboard drum). Solder or glue the two halves in place. Then run the shaft or axle rod, *C*, through the drum, soldering or glueing it at top and bottom. Bearings positioned as shown, *D*, will enable the drum assembly to turn more smoothly.

The vertical axle-shaft must now be extended by the addition of the spiraled wood drill, *E*. This can be fixed in line with a metal coupling, or it can be spot-welded to the shaft. (A friendly machine shop operator will do the job for you.) The spiral should then be housed inside a length of 1″ plastic plumbing pipe, *G*, with a plastic coupling at the top, *F*, and the bottom end of the tube left open. A simple wooden frame can then be devised to hold the whole assembly in place across the rim of a tank or a pool.

The wind will turn the rotor, *A*, causing the shaft, *C*, to turn. The spiral, *E*, will draw water up the tube, mixing it with air as it falls back to water level. Small holes drilled into the top of the plastic housing, *G*, will enable the water and air to mix more readily.

Perhaps you can think of other ways in which this small Savonius can be hooked up to do light work, such as winding kite string, stirring milkshakes, and so on.

What Is the Future of Wind Power?

Past attempts to use wind power to generate very large amounts of electricity for community use have run into trouble. The best known of the giant wind turbines was built in 1945 on a mountaintop in Vermont called Grandpa's Knob. The plant, Figure 64, had two blades, each over 80 feet long and weighing eight tons. It generated 1,250 kilowatts and withstood winds up to 115 mph for 23 days, until a comparatively light 25 mph wind tore one of its blades loose and hurled it 750 feet away. The

Fig. 64

project, which cost $1½ million to build, was abandoned, defeated by a fickle wind and perhaps by faulty engineering.

Since then, there has been much research on larger wind machines. Most promising are improvements on a vertical rotor that is about as old as the Savonius. The *Darrieus rotor*, Figure 65, resembles a giant eggbeater. Its thin airfoil blades are light and flexible enough to withstand the kind of gusty winds that destroyed the Grandpa's Knob turbine. The Darrieus is difficult to get started, but researchers in India have added two Savonius drums at the top to start the blades turning, and they predict that giant versions, hundreds of feet in diameter, will one day turn

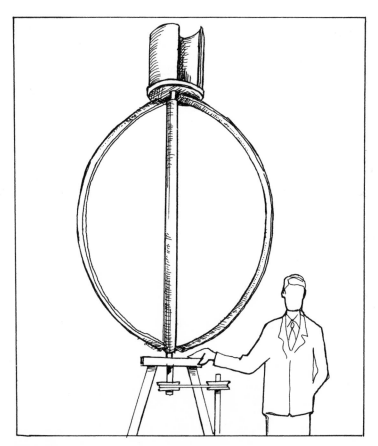

Fig. 65

India's powerful monsoon winds into the electricity badly needed by the oil-poor nation.

Meanwhile, in the United States, development of the propellered wind generator goes on, and scientists predict that large amounts of electricity will be produced by models of these machines in such wind-rich areas as the Oregon and Washington coasts, where several such projects have already begun. There is even a plan to mount wind generators in rows above our highways, which often provide ready-made channels to direct the wind. But again, there is a trade-off question: do we want the power badly enough to allow whirring machines to obscure our landscape?

Finally, a large, square-rigged sailing ship is being developed. Its rigging will be controlled by computer to save on labor costs and the considerable danger of climbing the mast to adjust sails. Here is a beautiful picture from the past now projected into the future: white-winged ships quietly and cleanly sailing our oceans. Do we really need to transport so much of our goods in fossil fuel-consuming and polluting jet planes and steam-turbine ships? Does a particular load of iron or lumber really have to get there so quickly, if the overall movement of materials is maintained at a steady pace and handled efficiently?

MADAME CURIE DISCOVERS RADIUM - 1898 -

5
NUCLEAR ENERGY

What Is Nuclear Energy?

Nuclear energy is produced from uranium mined from the earth. The heart of a nuclear power plant, Figure 68, is an array of long, thin rods filled with pellets of uranium fuel. As uranium atoms are split within these fuel elements, energy is produced to heat water circulating through the reactor. This heated water produces steam, and is carried to a turbine generator, which spins to produce electricity.

How Much Nuclear Power Is Available?

Uranium is a fossil fuel derived from pitchblende, the supply of which is limited. But nuclear proponents suggest that with more efficient new systems, the supply of nuclear power is almost limitless.

For a time, it was almost universally believed that nuclear energy was the best alternative to fossil fuels. Scientists predicted that this energy would be safe and "too cheap to meter," that is, so inexpensive that the producers would have trouble measuring use in order to charge their customers.

Since those hopeful predictions of the 1950s, under the

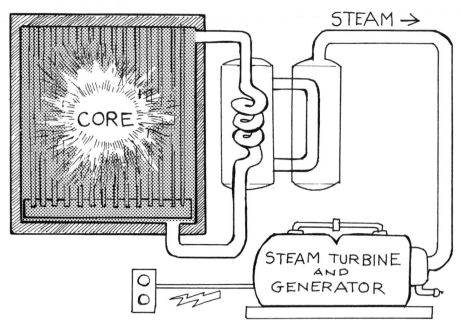

REACTOR

STEAM →

CORE

STEAM TURBINE
AND
GENERATOR

Fig. 68

guidance of the Atomic Energy Commission (AEC) and the Energy Research and Development Administration (ERDA), the U.S. government has spent $4 billion of the taxpayers' money on direct aid to the privately owned nuclear industry. Fifteen times that amount has been spent on military and atomic research, with all of that data available free of charge to the industry. In addition, the nuclear industry itself has spent many millions. And yet, with all that investment of what is really human labor, the nuclear energy industry has not succeeded in fulfilling its promises. Nuclear power is still not abundant, and what power is produced is definitely metered and sold by the power companies at the same rapidly increasing rates charged for energy produced by the burning of other, traditional fossil fuels.

Aren't All Energy Systems
Initially Expensive?

Yes, they are. At present, there are 55 operating nuclear plants is the United States. In the next 25 years, the nuclear industry expects to construct up to 1,000 new plants. They predict that by then the investment will begin to pay for itself and that nuclear power will be cheaper than energy produced by other systems.

But their cost figures do not include possible payment in human lives and damage to individual health and to the environment. A typical nuclear power plant contains an amount of radioactive material equal to the fallout from thousands of Hiroshima-size weapons. These plants are not as likely to explode like bombs as they are likely to leak radioactive material, as a result of a failure in the system. Much of this radioactive material is in the form of gas that could be carried by the wind for many miles. One such accident could kill as many as 45,000 people, cause $17 billion in property damage, and contaminate an area the size of Pennsylvania.

In addition, radioactive wastes are created when depleted nuclear fuel is removed from reactors. These wastes include strontium 90, cesium 137, and plutonium 239. A particle of plutonium the size of a grain of pollen causes lung cancer if inhaled. A typical nuclear power plant produces several hundred pounds of plutonium each year. The government estimates that by the end of this century, there will be 1 billion cubic feet of nuclear waste in the United States. That is enough to cover a one-foot deep four-lane highway, coast to coast.

Aren't There Safety Systems in Nuclear Plants?

Yes, there are. The basic safety system in nuclear plants is known as the "emergency core cooling system." If a pipe should break and the reactor's radioactive core threaten to overheat, it can be flooded with tons of water to cool it. But this water must reach the fuel within 60 seconds to prevent catastrophe. The system has never been tested under real conditions. The Union of Concerned Scientists reports that when the system was tested on small laboratory models, it consistently failed to function properly. In 1975 a fire threatened the Brown's Ferry Nuclear Station in Alabama. The core cooling system was not needed in that instance, but it could well have been. One authority admitted that a nuclear disaster had been averted by "sheer luck."

As for the long-term disposal of nuclear power plant wastes, no method has been proven effective. In 1973 115,000 gallons of radioactive waste leaked from a tank at the Atomic Energy Commission's facility in Hanford, Washington. Investigation revealed that the tank had been leaking for several weeks. No automatic alarm system had alerted anyone to the threat. Had the leaking materials reached an underground water channel, the contamination could have spread to wells and cisterns over hundreds of square miles.

What is more, such plutonium wastes can be used in making atomic bombs. Present safeguards may not be adequate to prevent a well-financed criminal or terrorist organization from stealing plutonium, manufacturing a bomb, and holding entire populations for ransom.

Aren't All Energy Systems Dangerous?

To some extent, yes. Train wrecks, mine cave-ins, fires caused by faulty electrical wiring, explosions of gas mains and tanks—all have taken many lives over the years. Even millions of dollars in property are destroyed every year by the careless use of a simple energy system like the common wood stove.

Has Nuclear Energy for Peaceful Purposes Destroyed Property or Lives?

Not directly. However, recent government studies reveal that of several hundred nuclear workers exposed to levels of radiation once considered safe, death from cancer-related causes was 20 percent higher than average.

Radioactive substances remain dangerous virtually forever.

It takes plutonium half a million years to lose its killing power. One accident, and children living within 50 miles downwind from the site would very likely die of lung or thyroid cancer for the ensuing 500,000 years! Multiply this by the projected 1,000 nuclear reactors in the United States alone by 1980, and you have the potential for half a billion deaths and an uninhabitable landscape. That would be more damage than has resulted from the use of all the other forms of energy since the first man-made fire a million or more years ago.

Doesn't Nuclear Energy Have the Potential to Produce More Energy Than Any Other Method?

Some experts—almost all of them present or former employees of the nuclear industry—believe that the future lies with another kind of nuclear system based on nuclear fusion. This is the harnessing of heat thrown off by the fusing of hydrogen isotopes, deuterium, and tritium. The basic materials can be extracted from sea water, they say, and therefore might be regarded as a limitless source of energy. One assistant administrator of ERDA, believes that hydrogen isotopes can be made to fuse in a way that produces more energy than is consumed. The first fusion reactor, scheduled to be built at Princeton University in 1981, will cost at least $228 million and will require a process temperature of 60 million degrees centigrade. This means that tremendous power will be required to operate the facility. But the power produced, predict ERDA experts, will again be too cheap to meter.

One is reminded of the medieval alchemists, who believed that lead could be turned into gold. As it turns out, they were right. It can be done by bombarding the lead with an atomic reactor. But, to produce one ounce of that gold costs approximately 10,000 times as much as it does to purchase natural gold on the open market.

Nuclear fusion will pose similar dangers to life and the environment as do the present methods.

We have not included instructions for a model of a nuclear device in this book for obvious reasons.

117

Fig. 69

6
OTHER ALTERNATIVES

What Are the Other Energy Alternatives?

As you can see from Figures 69 and 70, some alternatives are questionable, some downright absurd. But there is one general alternative that deserves the most serious consideration: conservation.

All over the world, but particularly in our abundant industrial society, energy is being unnecessarily wasted, both in small and large ways. A badly designed and installed wood stove sends at least half of its heat straight up a chimney. Fifty percent of the energy produced by *all* of our big power plants is lost in the process of transmission, and because of mechanical inefficiencies and incomplete combustion. There are promising old and new devices that can help us make better use of our remaining fossil fuels. There are other inventions to produce power from the wastes themselves. There are minor sacrifices we can make and devices we can utilize to personally cut down this waste. In fact, you can begin right now with a stack of old newspapers, some common chemicals, and a little muscle power.

ANIMAL POWER ?

The illustration above shows how the double dog power can be used in operating a cream separator; when the separator is not in use and you desire to churn connect it to tumbling rod sent with machine. A corn sheller, fan mill or sawing machine, can be connected by belt from balance wheel. Separators require a high gear and for this purpose we recommend our steel pulley, 3½ by 36 inches, this we can furnish at $6.00 extra. If iron coupling rod and coupling as shown in illustration are desired to connect and run cream separator, we can furnish them at $3.00 extra.

Fig. 70

HOW TO MAKE FIREPLACE LOGS FROM NEWSPAPERS

For the simplest and cheapest newspaper logs, you will need a stack of newspapers, some light wire or heavy string, and perhaps a length of broomstick. Open the newspapers and layer them until you have a stack about three inches thick. Soak them in water or other fluid (see below), then roll them as tightly as you can. Using the length of broomstick as a core makes it a little easier to roll the paper, but it will leave a hole if it is removed. If you do not have enough broomstick to leave each length in its log, roll without it. Then tie the log with wire or cord, spacing the ties about every three to five inches. (Wire is better than cord for the ties, but it will remain after the log has burned.) Dry the rolled paper logs thoroughly in the sun, then burn them in the fireplace as you would any other log.

For faster burning fuel, soak the paper logs with charcoal lighter or kerosene. Be sure to do this out of doors and *never use gasoline*. If you want the logs to burn colorfully for a festive occasion, such as Christmas, add one of the following chemicals to the water in the ratio of one cup of coloring substance to three cups or more of water. *Wear rubber gloves and do not let the chemicals get into your eyes.* For bright green, use boric acid. For yellow, common table salt. For green, copper sulfate. For blue, copper chloride. For red, strontium chloride. For crimson, lithium chloride. For orange, calcium chloride. For yellow-orange, baking soda. Chlorides and sulfates are what you want; *do not use nitrates or chlorates.* Most of the substances are available at any well-stocked drugstore or through one of the chemical supply houses listed in the Yellow Pages of your phone directory.

Figure 71 shows a homemade log press you can make. The front plate, *A,* is cut from plywood and secured with iron shelf braces that move in the slots, *D,* to press the roll against the permanently fixed back plate. Wing nuts help hold the front plate in place while you tie the rolled paper. These lengths of wire or cord have been previously threaded through the slots in the plates and under the roll for easier tying. A manufactured paper-log-rolling device is available from Aviterra Corp., Box 34275, Bethesda, Maryland, 20034. Write for details.

Put your logs on the fire only after the blaze is well started and the fireplace draft is drawing well.

Can a Few Newspaper Logs Help Solve the Energy Crisis?

The answer to that is yes, in a way. We will leave the explanation of this for the end of the chapter. In the meantime, let's swing back to the larger picture and the possibilities for improving the efficiency of the giant power plants.

How Can Power Plants Operate More Efficiently?

In our present power plants, it takes three units of high-temperature energy (from fossil fuels) to produce one unit of

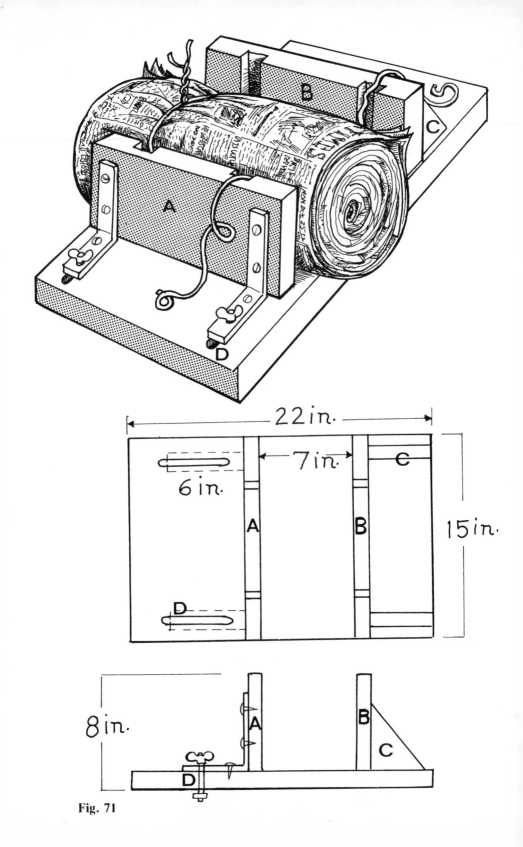

Fig. 71

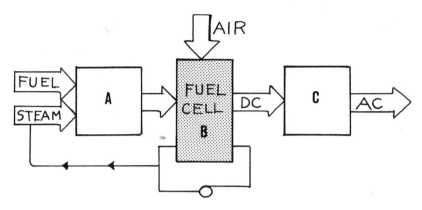

Fig. 72

equivalent electrical energy. But electricity is a very handy tool; it's easy to store and transport, and is clean and efficient to use. One of several available means of making electricity more efficiently from available fuels is the fuel cell.

The *fuel cell* is a battery-like device that generates a DC current by chemical reaction. Fuel cells have been used successfully to power space satellites by converting hydrogen and oxygen into electricity. Figure 72 is a simplified diagram of a fuel-cell power plant. The reformer section, *A*, processes hydrocarbon for fuel cell use. The power section, *B*, converts processed fuel and air into DC power. The inverter, *C*, changes DC to AC. Scientists predict that by 1985, fuel-cell power plants in the U.S. will be saving the equivalent of 275,000 barrels of oil a day. Not only can our methods for producing large amounts of electricity be more efficient, but our use of small amounts at home can be more efficient as well.

How Can Home Use of Energy Be More Efficient?

The most direct way is to stop using so much. We said the average American home uses from 400 to 550 kwh per month. In actual fact, many homes use much more. Here are some

123

representative electrical appliances, together with the kwh consumed by each per month during average use:

Appliance	kwh per month
75-watt light bulb	90
Clothes dryer	80
Clock	1.5
Dishwasher	28
Air conditioner	105
Iron	13
Kitchen range	102
Sewing machine	1
Radio	7.5
Color television	37.5
Washing machine (automatic)	5.5
Food freezer	76
Toaster	3
Hair dryer	0.5
Water heater	373
Total:	923.5 kwh per month

The total looks overpowering, doesn't it? But do we really need that air conditioner? Can't we go back to washing dishes by hand? If we change those 75-watt bulbs to 40-watt bulbs, the monthly light bill is reduced by 42 kwh per month. If we dry our clothes in the sun whenever possible, we can cut one third off the kwh consumption of the dryer. A nonautomatic washer uses 1.5 kwh less than an automatic machine. A black-and-white television set uses 8.5 kwh less than a color set. Even that hurts, doesn't it? And we've only lowered consumption to 712.5 kwh.

Can you think of anything else you could easily give up? The answer probably is no. If the house is also electrically heated, consumption can be reduced by the addition of extra insulation, particularly under the roof, and by double-glazing or adding storm windows. But this does not reduce the cost of running all those appliances. This is where other alternatives come in. They still will not solve our problem, but if there is any solution, it lies in the integrated systems discussed in Chapter Seven. But wouldn't it be helpful to replace that energy-gobbling electric kitchen range with a wood or sawdust stove?

How Can a Wood Stove Solve the Energy Shortage?

It can't solve it entirely. By now we know we are not going to solve the shortage with any one alternative, and wood is no exception. On the other hand, wood is unlike the fossil fuels in that it is a renewable resource. A new tree can be grown in five to 50 years, while it takes coal, oil, and natural gas hundreds of thousands of years to form. Wood produces fewer pollutants than most other fuels. By burning it directly in your own stove, you will be saving that 50 percent loss in the production and transmission of electricity. For that reason, wood is especially efficient for space-heating a home.

It is true that the world is using wood faster than it grows it, despite sustained yield programs for the replanting and controlled harvesting of trees. It is also true that it takes up to five acres of carefully managed woodlot to heat a home over the years, and most people don't have that much land. Furthermore, although wood-burning stoves add almost none of the deadly sulfur dioxide emitted by coal and gasoline into the air of our cities, wood stoves would still add to that pollution. But wood is still plentiful in many areas of the world, and many trees remain unharvested and go to rot. An acre of woodlot will yield a cord of wood (a pile 8' × 4' × 4') every year in broken and fallen limbs alone, and a cord of wood yields as much heat energy as half a ton of coal.

In addition, this country wastes a tremendous amount of wood. The U.S. Forest Service estimates that as much as 30 percent of the rubbish discarded by the cities is reusable wood material. The proper harvesting of wood does not do nearly as much damage to the landscape as does the drilling, digging, and strip-mining of fossil fuels. And you can save the labor of

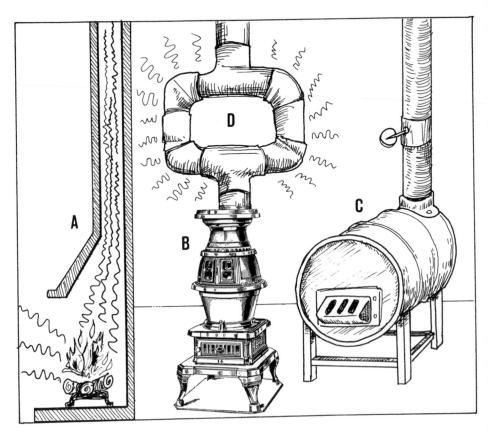

Fig. 73

production by collecting or cutting the wood yourself—if you have the time and are willing to do the work.

What Is the Best Way to Burn Wood?

Wood is most efficiently burned in an automatic airtight stove, called a *complete combustion burner.* Most stone or brick fireplaces are inefficient and send half or more of the available heat up chimneys. The old-fashioned, potbellied stove, shown in Figure 73, *B,* is better because it at least radiates heat from its entire surface. A serviceable stove, called the *Yukon,* can be

made from a recycled 55-gallon drum, as shown, *C*. The door
and legs can be made from sheet metal or cast iron parts sold at
stove supply outlets. A second drum can be added above the first
to radiate heat that would otherwise be lost up the chimney.
Another method of salvaging chimney heat from almost any
wood stove is the extra loop of pipe added above the stove, as in
D.

But the best wood stove is an entirely enclosed, complete
combustion unit like the one in Figure 74. The air intake

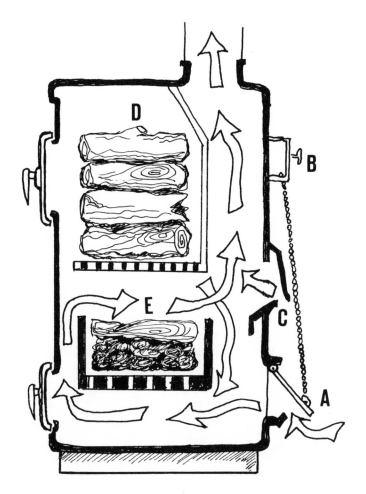

Fig. 74

damper, *A*, is controlled by an automatic thermostat, *B*. It closes if the stove overheats; it lets more air in if the fire gets too low. The secondary intake system, *C*, captures unburned gases that would usually go up the chimney, and circulates them back through the fire a second time, *E*. Automatic stoves like this can maintain a fire for from 12 to 24 hours and can be combined with backup oil or gas systems.

Sawdust is a much neglected by-product of the wood industry, and heaps of it can be found going to rot beside lumber mills and carpenter shops. You can heat a garage, a shop, or a greenhouse with a homemade stove that will put usually wasted sawdust to practical use.

HOW TO BUILD A SAWDUST STOVE

Although the cost of materials for this stove is very low, it does require special metal-working skills. It might be worthwhile to have it made in a sheet metal shop, because it will burn up to 18 hours on 30 pounds or less of inexpensive sawdust.

The drum, top, damper door, and legs are made of medium-gauge sheet steel, available at a metal supplier or at a junk yard. The stove body, (Figure 75, *A)* consists of a simple metal tube with a double bottom. There is a two-inch hole in the center of the extra bottom, *c*. The stove is loaded from the top, through the hinged door, *a*. Gases and smoke are drawn off by the stovepipe at the rear, *b*. Air is admitted through the damper door at the bottom, *d*, and ashes are removed through the same opening.

To load the stove, the tapered wooden shaft, *B*, is placed down through the center of the drum, with its end fitted snugly through the hole, *c*, at the bottom. Sawdust is then sprinkled into the drum and packed around the shaft. A few inches of sawdust are poured, then sprinkled with water and patted down tightly. Then another layer of sawdust is loaded in, moistened, and patted down, until about 2½ feet of packed sawdust fills the

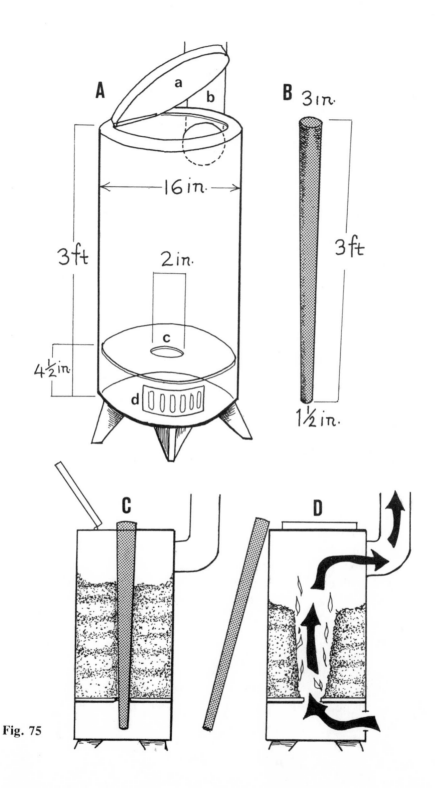

A
a
b
16 in.
3 ft
2 in.
c
4½ in.
d

B 3 in.
3 ft
1½ in.

C

D

Fig. 75

stove. The shaft is then carefully lifted out, leaving an open chimney at the core of the sawdust pack, as shown, *D*. Crumpled newspaper is pushed through the damper door, *D*, and lighted. The flames will ignite the sides of the sawdust "chimney," causing the sawdust pack to burn from the inside out, that is, from the walls of the "chimney" toward the outer surface of the drum. Because the heat does not directly contact the drum walls until the end of the burning cycle, the metal need not be thick, and will last a long time. If the sawdust has been packed carefully, the fire will burn with a steady, smoldering glow, intense heat, and very little smoke.

However, if the exhaust pipe is not tightly fitted at the back, or the chimney pipe is not long enough, heavy winds can cause a reverse draft that will drive the gases and smoke back down the drum and out through the damper vent. These fumes can be deadly, and for that reason the stove must not be used where anybody is sleeping. But a tight exhaust pipe and a chimney pipe that rises well above the roof peak will insure that no dangerous backup takes place.

Are There Other Wasted By-products That Can Be Turned into Energy?

Yes. Manure. When organic material decays, it produces useful by-products: gases and solid materials. If it decays in the open where oxygen can get to it, it produces common fertilizer and biogases, mostly ammonia and carbon dioxide. But if the decaying organic materials are sealed in a container where little or no oxygen is present, it produces high-grade fertilizer and a combustible biogas composed mostly of carbon dioxide and *methane*. This gas can be burned for cooking, heating, and even the production of electricity. The device that produces methane is called a *digester*.

Figure 76 shows a simple *anaerobic* (oxygen-free) methane digester. A *slurry* (a soupy blend of sewage), chopped up plant material, and even chopped newspaper is fed into the inlet, *A*, until it nearly fills the sealed chamber. If the interior of the chamber is maintained at 75° to 90° F, bacteria and microbes

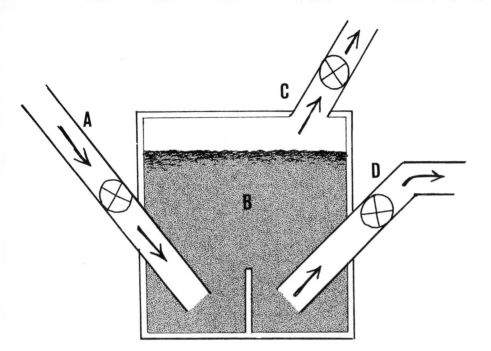

Fig. 76

begin to "digest" the slurry material. After a few days, burnable biogas begins to exit from the outlet, *B.* The heavier materials settle to the bottom, where they become a sludge composed of wastes and *supernatant,* or highly nutritive fertilizer, which is then withdrawn through exit *C.*

The process of maintaining, loading, and unloading a digester can be fully automated, or it can be done by hand. A number of large sewage-processing plants in this country and abroad are run entirely on the methane gas produced by their digesters, and some even produce additional gas and fertilizer for use elsewhere. Hundreds of modern homesteaders have built their own digesters from such recycled materials as old oil drums, tractor tire tubes, and used plumbing pipes.

Can I Make My Own Methane?

Yes, however, please use *caution:* METHANE GAS IS HIGHLY INFLAMMABLE AND CAN BE EXPLOSIVE.

While this experiment has been performed without harm in many high-school science classes, it must be done with *adult supervision*, preferably *expert* supervision. The best way is to suggest it to your science teacher.

HOW TO MAKE A TABLETOP METHANE DIGESTER

To make the small digester shown in Figure 77, you will need:

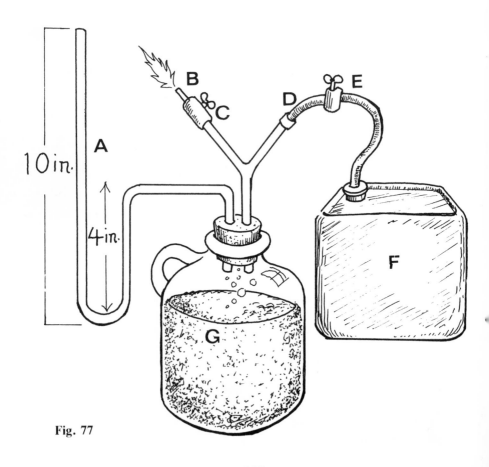

Fig. 77

1   1-gallon glass cider jug
1   gas container (a plastic bag, plastic milk jug, or metal
    oil can, thoroughly cleaned)
1   1½' length of rubber or plastic tubing
2   tubing clamps
1   two-hole rubber stopper to fit the cider jug
1   glass tube about 24" long
1   glass "Y"
    about five pounds of manure

The glass tubing, glass "Y", rubber stopper, and clamps can be obtained from a chemical supply house, but may also be available in your science class at school.

The first step is to make a *manometer*, the U-shaped length of tubing shown, *A*, in Figure 77. Partly filled with water, it will indicate when the digester is producing gas, and it will also act as a safety valve, blowing out the water and letting the gas escape if the pressure becomes dangerous. The manometer's shape is formed by heating the tubing over a Bunsen burner, as your science teacher can demonstrate. Next, make a burner tip, *B*, by drawing out one end of a length of glass tubing. (Again, let your science teacher show you how to do this.) Make the tip at least two inches long to avoid any backflash, and attach it to one extension of the glass "Y" with a short piece of rubber tubing and clamp, as shown, *C*.

The other branch of the "Y" feeds directly to the gas collector, *F*, through a length of rubber tubing with a clamp, *E*, to pinch the tubing and seal it.

Once the digester is assembled, you are ready to place a slurry of manure in the cider jug. A mixture of droppings and litter from the floor of a chicken house is best, with cow manure next in value. Horse manure is the least productive. Mix the manure with water to form a soupy slurry and pour it into the jug, filling it to about four inches below the stopper. It will foam at first; be sure to keep the foam out of the tubing.

Keep the digester at a temperature between 90° and 100° F. It can be placed within five feet of a closed furnace, but *do not place it near an open flame.* Pour water into the manometer tube, *A*, until at least four inches of its U bend is full. Close the clamp on the tube leading to the gas collector, *E*. After two days or more, water propelled up the long arm of the manometer will signal that a quantity of gas is being produced. This first gas will be mostly carbon dioxide and will not burn. To test it, open the clamp, *C*, at the burner tip and hold a lighted match to it. If the gas does not burn, allow it to escape, then reseal the clamp. Continue testing daily until a match held at the tip ignites the escaping gas, showing that it is mostly methane. Production of burnable methane can take two weeks or more, depending on the acid conditions in the slurry. Once methane is being produced, it should continue doing so from one to three months. When no more gas is being produced, take the jug outside and pour the residue contents into a flower garden or mulch bed. This is top-grade fertilizer, and it represents alternative conservation at its best.

Is a Methane Digester Practical for Home Use?

The answer is a qualified yes. It takes one-third more methane to give the same heat value as natural gas, and most gas appliances require some conversion to burn methane. A small digester, producing 50 cubic feet of biogas per day, will help to lower the average yearly natural gas bill and will produce a sizable savings over commercial fertilizer. A large digester can also save the cost of installing a septic tank, since all organic wastes are being recycled.

Home-size digesters require a lot of tending, but the cost goes up with automatic controls. It takes the waste from eight adults or 60 chickens to provide enough gas to cook the meals of a single person per day. On the other hand, the price of natural gas is going up every day and may soon be out of control.

Obviously, small-scale methane production is of little use to city dwellers. But a digester could provide a worthwhile percentage of the cooking needs of a group of people or families operating in an integrated rural ecosystem, as discussed in Chapter Seven.

Can Methane Be Used to Drive an Automobile?

Yes, but at a cost so high that it would not be economical even if gasoline were to triple in price. The same goes for wood- and alcohol-powered cars. In the end, the only solution to the automobile problem will be the introduction of small electric cars, combined with a complete rededication to mass transportation systems—railroads and subways.

How Else Can We Salvage Wasted Fuels?

We can recycle our garbage. In 1973 the United States produced 135 million tons of garbage. By 1985 that amount will probably increase to 200 million tons. At present, most of it is dumped into landfills and covered with a thin layer of earth that does little to stop it from contaminating ground water supplies. Of the garbage thrown away in 1973, 35 million tons were burnable paper and plastic, which contained the energy potential of 150 million barrels of oil. We also threw away 12 million tons of steel, 1 million tons of aluminum, and 200,000 tons of copper. The 38 billion glass containers that were buried under landfills could have been ground up and mixed with stones to make an excellent highway surfacing material.

Fortunately, the federal and local governments are moving rapidly to save these valuable fuels and metals. If the big cities in your state do not already have resource-recovery plants, they will undoubtedly have them within the next decade or so.

There are several methods of resource recovery. One of them is the Monsanto Langard gas pyrolysis system used in Baltimore. A simplified version of the system is shown in Figure 78. Garbage dumped by the truck, *1*, drops through a shredder, *2*, which turns it to pulp. The pulp releases combustible gases. These gases are burned in the afterburner, *C*, releasing heat which is recovered as steam. The steam, in turn, is used to run a steam turbine to produce electricity. Metals are also extracted from the pulp by magnets, *6*.

135

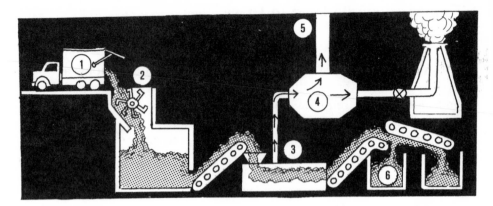

Fig. 78

You can, of course, do a similar job with no machinery other than your hands and a couple of boxes—one to hold metal refuse to be recycled for home use or taken to recycling depots for return to industry. (Alcoa Aluminum Company has set up such depots for aluminum cans in some cities. For details, contact Alcoa or the Environmental Protection Agency office in the nearest large city, or write to the EPA, Washington, D.C., 20460.) The second box is for paper refuse for starting the wood stove, for feeding a methane digester, and for being chopped into mulch for the garden, or rolled into paper logs for the fireplace.

Tell Us Now, How Can a Few Paper Logs Solve the Energy Crisis?

That will be up to you and everybody else in the world. If every one of the 4 billion men, women, and children on this planet could be persuaded to heat their evening drink tonight with just four pounds of "logs" made from recycled newspaper, the resulting savings in coal-produced electricity would be enough to run 1,248,000 modern homes all day tomorrow. That is more than enough energy to meet the daily needs of the entire population of Bangalore, the ninth largest city in India.

A drop in the bucket, you say? True, but that is how a bucket is filled—drop by drop.

In the end, conservation and sharing will be the only answer to our energy problems. It is true that a more rational and humane worldwide social and economic system is needed to make conservation have its full impact. But in the meantime, somebody has to make a start.

Fig. 79

7

INTEGRATED SYSTEMS

What Is an Integrated System?

An *integrated system* is an energy system designed to combine alternatives in a way that will produce more power than if the alternatives were used separately. Hopefully, a good integrated system will also do the minimum possible damage to the environment and its resources. The great advantage of a well-thought-out integrated system is that certain alternatives have *synergistic relationships:* that is, each supplies the other with a missing need, with the result that they are more effective in combination than they would be separately.

An example is shown in Figure 81. Recall that the slurry in a methane digester must be kept at a temperature above 75° F for the mixture to produce gas. Here, the solar collector delivers heat to the heat storage tank, and some of that heat is routed back through a heat exchanger to the inside of the digester to heat the slurry. At another point in the integrated pattern, the pond receives supernatant fertilizer from the digester with which to feed its tiny water plants and, perhaps, some fish. At the same time, it produces feed for the chickens, which in turn produce manure for the digester. The pond even sends some of its own biofuels back to help feed the digester.

How many other synergistic or mutual-help relationships can you find in the diagram?

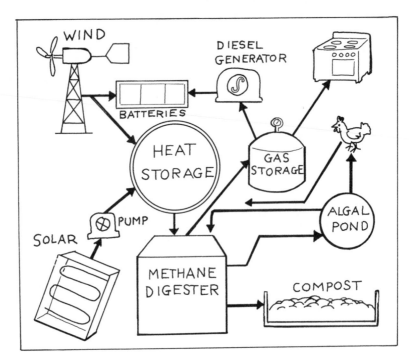

Fig. 81

Are Integrated Systems a New Idea?

Not really. Since the beginning of agriculture, men have been integrating their use of tools, labor, and by-products. The subsistence farm of early rural America was sometimes a nearly perfect combination of synergistic effects. A windmill or a waterwheel brought up water for the livestock; the cows ate grass and hay, and gave milk and meat; the horses plowed the fields; their manure was used to enrich next year's hay crop; the trees shaded the house and animals and dropped their leaves for compost, and so on.

Can I Build an Integrated System?

Yes, by combining some of the alternative energy devices described in this book. Figures 82 and 83 show one possible combination, modeled after one of the *ecosystems* (ecologically balanced systems) developed by the New Alchemy Institute of Woods Hole, Massachusetts (see Appendix).

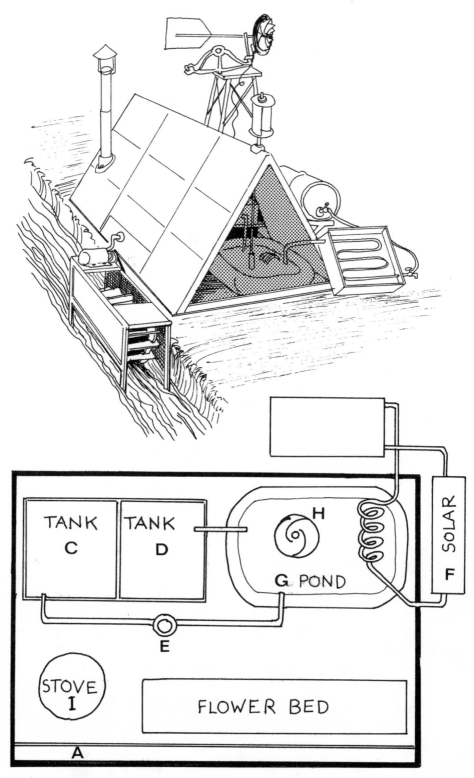

TANK C

TANK D

H

G. POND

F SOLAR

E

STOVE I

FLOWER BED

A

Fig. 82

HOW TO DEVELOP AN INTEGRATED AQUACULTURE SYSTEM

The *aquaculture system*—a solar-heated, wind-powered combination of greenhouse and backyard fish farm—can produce edible plants and fish in a moderate climate with no direct consumption of fossil fuels and with little harm to the environment. It is housed in and around our 9′ × 12′, A-frame greenhouse. Figure 82 gives a general view and the floor plan. Figure 83 gives a cross-sectional view, as seen from one side of the greenhouse.

Solar energy is harvested by the thermosiphoning wall of the greenhouse, *A*, and used to grow plants, as well as to heat the pond system, *C, D, G*. Heat for night use is stored in drums on which the double tank rests, *X*, and in plastic containers stowed in unused corners. Wind power helps the bicycle wind generator, *B*, run a small lamp for light and a small amount of additional heat. Our other wind generator could be used to operate a small three-volt pump, *E*, available from Edmond Scientific Company (see Appendix). This pump raises water from the pond, *G*, back up to the double tanks, *C, D*, with the water then allowed to trickle through the tanks and back down to the pond. Or, if the system is located at the side of a small stream, our undershot waterwheel could be geared to run a plastic "jackrabbit" pump for the same purpose (see Appendix under Suppliers).

Our solar collector and hot water system warms the pond water with the immersion of a copper-coil heat exchanger in the pond water.

The Savonius rotor, *H*, located on the roof and equipped with a long shaft, helps agitate the water in the pond to provide the fish with additional oxygen. Our sawdust stove, *I*, is installed inside the greenhouse to act as a backup heat source. Or you might use a small wood stove that burns newspaper logs.

The aquaculture (water culture) system consists of the pond, *G*, and the double tank, *C, D*. The double tank is made of wood and has two compartments, each lined with black plastic film. The first compartment, *C*, contains a bed of crushed stone or

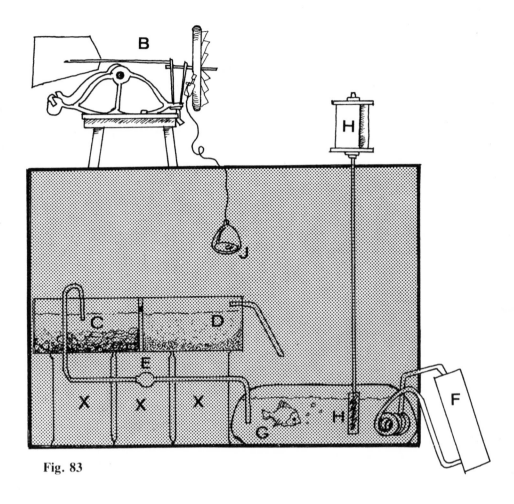

Fig. 83

clam shells, which help filter fish wastes out of the water that has been pumped from the pond. At the same time, it uses these wastes to promote the growth of microbiological nitrates, which can then be recycled to fertilize the plants. Some of them can also be fed to the fish.

Water filtered from the first compartment to the second compartment, *D*, then contains nutrients which will help promote the growth of microscopic algae. The algae are then allowed to overflow into pond *G*, where they help feed the fish. Pond *G* is a small plastic wading pool, resting on the floor of the greenhouse.

The best species of fish for aquaculture is an oriental breed called Tilapia, but this species is not yet readily available in the United States. Because bluegills, a variety of sunfish, do not thrive for long in small bodies of water, we switched from them to goldfish. Goldfish are a variety of carp—a common food fish in the Orient. Although we have not yet been able to bring ourselves to eat them, they thrived in the system. For more information about aquaculture, write to the New Alchemy Institute and other sources listed in the Appendix.

You can probably devise your own integrated, alternative energy system. The aim is to interconnect all units in order to make maximum use of the potential of each.

But Isn't Human Society Already an Integrated System?

It certainly is. The problem is that it is inefficient and often environmentally destructive and detrimental to the lives of

Fig. 84

human beings. As it stands now, an underdeveloped nation supplies raw materials to an industrialized nation, which turns the materials into fabricated products. The products, in turn, help to raise the standard of living of the people of the underdeveloped nation. However, because the industrialized nations own the means of production, they are able to exact more than their proportionate share of health, life, and leisure from the system. Some forms of alternative energy are not morally acceptable, see Figure 84.

But this will most likely be brought into better balance within the next century. Then, the challenge will be to make the system less wasteful and more productive for all.

In the meantime, we must each ask ourselves: what am *I* going to do about it?

COMMON METRIC EQUIVALENTS
AND CONVERSIONS

Approximate

1 inch	= 25 millimeters
1 foot	= 0.3 meter
1 yard	= 0.9 meter
1 square inch	= 6.5 square centimeters
1 square foot	= 0.09 square meter
1 square yard	= 0.8 square meter
1 millimeter	= 0.04 inch
1 meter	= 3.3 feet
1 meter	= 1.1 yards
1 square centimeter	= 0.16 square inch

Accurate to Parts Per Million

inches × 25.4	= millimeters
feet × 0.3048	= meters
yards × 0.9144	= meters
square inches × 6.4516	= square centimeters
square feet × 0.092903	= square meters
square yards × 0.836127	= square meters

Temperature Conversion

The Celsius scale (C), often called the centigrade scale, is derived from the Fahrenheit scale by the following formula:

$$C = \frac{5(F\text{-}32)}{9}$$

APPENDIX

Listings are not arranged alphabetically, but in order of considered relative value to the beginner.

BOOKS

General

Other Homes and Garbage, J. Leckie, G. Masters, H. Whitehouse and L. Young; Sierra Club Books, San Francisco, 1975. Paperback. An overall treatment of the alternatives; conservative and technically well-informed, with sections on architecture, wind and water generation of electricity, solar heating, waste-handling systems, water supply, agriculture, and aquaculture.
Alternative Sources of Energy, Sandy Eccli, ed., Continuum Books, Seabury Press, New York, 1975. Paperback. Fun to read. Contains an interesting section on wave power.
Energy Primer, Portola Institute, Menlo Park, Cal., 1974. Paperback. Provides sources and includes informative articles, particularly on wood and aquaculture.

Handbook of Homemade Power, Mother Earth News,
Hendersonville, N.C., 1974. Paperback. Contains do-it-
yourself alternative projects.
The Last Whole Earth Catalogue, Portola Institute, Menlo
Park, Cal., 1971. Paperback. Provides sources for books,
equipment, and materials.

Solar

The Solar Home Book, Bruce Anderson and Michael
Riordan, Cheshire Books, Harrisville, N.H., 1976. Paper-
back. Summary of low- and medium-tech solar systems, with
emphasis on solar architecture.
Direct Use of the Sun's Energy, Farrington Daniels, Ballan-
tine Books, New York, 1964. Paperback. Summary of solar
history and possibilities.
Solar Energy, Franklyn M. Branley, T. Y. Crowell Co.,
New York, 1975.
Solar Greenhouse Design, Construction, and Operation,
Rick Fisher and Bill Yanda, John Muir Publications, Santa
Fe, Cal., 1976. Paperback.
Solar Cells and Photocells, Rufus P. Turner, Howard W.
Sams & Co., Bobbs-Merrill, New York, 1975. Paperback.
Solar Age Catalogue, SolarVision, Inc., Port Jervis, N.Y.,
1977. Paperback. Contains listings of solar suppliers, and
technical articles.
Solar Energy Catalogue, Nick Nicholson and Bruce David-
son, Renewable Energy Publications, Frenchtown, N.J.,
1977. Paperback. Presents plans for eight solar homes.

Water

Harnessing Water Power for Home Energy, Dermot
McGuigan, Garden Way Publishing Co., Charlotte, Vt.,
1978. Paperback. Introduction to water power.
Windmills and Watermills, John Reynolds, Praeger Pub-
lishers, New York, 1970. Paperback. A history of water and

wind power, with schematic drawings of the workings of old-time mills.

Pebble Collecting and Polishing, Edward Fletcher, Sterling Publishing Co., New York, 1973. Information for use with an undershot wheel rock tumbler.

See also books listed under General, above.

Wind

Harnessing the Wind for Home Energy, Dermot McGuigan, Garden Way Publishing Co., Charlotte, Vt., 1978. Paperback. An introduction to wind power.

See also books under General, particularly the first and third listed. See also, *Windmills and Waterwheels.*

Integrated

Journal of the New Alchemists, New Alchemy Institute, P.O. Box 432, Woods Hole, Mass., 1977. Paperback. Summaries of bioculture and aquaculture systems, particularly journals number 2 and 3.

See also, *Other Homes and Garbage, Energy Primer,* and *Alternative Sources of Energy,* in that order.

MAGAZINES

Popular Science. Boulder, Colorado. (Monthly) Presentation of both high- and low-tech energy innovations.

Mother Earth News. Hendersonville, N.C. (Bimonthly) Represents the back-to-the-earth movement with direct-value do-it-yourself projects, emphasis on low-tech and integrated systems and small-scale agriculture.

Harrowsmith. Camden House, Ontario, Canada. (Bimonthly) Similar to *Mother Earth News* but for *Canadian* readers, with emphasis on small-scale farming.

Solar Age. SolarVision, Inc., Port Jervis, N.Y. (Monthly) Emphasis on solar energy.

Scientific American. (Monthly) Technical coverage of specific energy matters.

CoEvolution Quarterly. POINT, Sausalito, Cal. (Quarterly) By editors of the *Whole Earth Catalogue.*

The Lapidary Journal. P.O. Box 80937, San Diego, Cal. 92138. Sources for suppliers of rock tumblers and polishing materials.

SUPPLIERS

General

Edmond Scientific Company, 675 Edscorp Building, Barrington, N.J. 08007. Source for low-cost photovoltaic cells, parabolic reflectors, Fresnel lenses and other solar equipment, wind chargers, small water pumps, and many other items. A 162-page catalogue is available, write for details. Edmond also sells a model of a water pumping windmill and plans for building a model of an old-fashioned Dutch mill.

Solar

A-Z Solar Products, 200 E. 26th Street, Minneapolis, Minn. 55404. Source for solar components: photovoltaic cells, and parts for flat-plate collectors such as fiberglass-reinforced collector cover plates, solar reflector foil, heat transfer cements, high-absorbency black paint, complete water heating systems and their components. Catalogue available, write for details.

Kalwall Corporation, 1111 Candia Road, Manchester, N.H. 03103. Sun-Lite fiberglass cover panels for solar collectors. Write for prices.

Calmac Corporation, Box 710, Englewood, N.J. 07631. Manufacturers of rolled plastic collectors.

See also *Energy Primer, Solar Age Catalogue,* and *The Solar Home Book.*

Water

Independent Power Developers, Box 1467, Noxon, Montana 59853. Small impulse turbines and other equipment for production of domestic electricity from high-head mountain streams. Catalogue available, write for details.
Westward Mouldings Ltd., Greenhill Works, Delaware Road, Bunnislake, Cornwall, England. Fiberglass water-wheels 8 to 20 feet in diameter. Expensive.
For other suppliers, see also *Other Homes and Garbage, Handbook of Homemade Power, Energy Primer,* and *Harnessing Water Power for Home Energy.*

Wind

Boston Wind Company, 2 Maston Court, Charlestown, Mass. 02129. New and used wind generators and a quarterly newsletter.
Energy Alternatives, Inc., 69 Amherst Road, Leverett, Mass. 01054. Agents for Dunlite, Jacobs and Aero-Power wind chargers. Also offers designs.
See also under Books *Handbook of Homemade Power, Energy Primer,* and *Harnessing the Wind for Home Energy.*

Aquaculture

J. M. Malone and Son Enterprises, P.O. Box 158, Lanoke, Arkansas 72086. Sells grass carp and is breeding Tilapia. For the serious aquaculturist.
Perry Minnow Farm, Rt. 1, Box 128-C, Windsor, Virginia 23487. Sells Israeli carp.
Sporty's Tool Shop, Clermont County Airport, Batavia, Ohio 45103. Source for the Jackrabbit Pump; also offers a miniature wind sock. Write for a catalogue.

INDEX

absorber panel, 13, 16, 34, 36, 41, 43
active systems, 19, 33
alternating current (AC), 78, 97
alternative energy, 3, 4, 5, 7, 16, 66, 82, 113–118
alternator, 78, 95, 103
anaerobic digester (methane), 130
annular wind wheel, 94
anti-freeze, 34, 38, 46
aquaculture, 142–44
artificial head (water), 68
auxiliary heater, 34

battery charger, 47
bicycle wind plant, 98–102
black absorber, 16, 29
blower, 36
breast (water) wheel, 66

calibration, wind gauge, 90
coal, 4, 5
collector
  solar, 14, 33, 34, 41
  concentrating, 49
  flat-basin, 38
  flat-plate, 33, 34
complete combustion burner, 125
conduction, 18
conservation, 119–44
construction, solar home, 21
convection, 18, 25, 38

cooker, solar, 49
cover plate, 34, 35

dam, 4, 63, 68
Darrieus (wind) rotor, 109
desert still, 56
digester, methane, 130
direct current (DC), 78, 97
distillation, 12, 55
doghouse, solar, 59

ecosystem, 140
electricity
  home use, 103, 123–24
  hydroelectric, 63
  nuclear, 113–18
  storage, 97
  wind, 89, 94, 96, 103
Elektra wind plant, 103
energy, alternative
  defined, 3, 5, 7
  geothermal, 82
  kinetic, 66
  nuclear, 113-18
  storage, 16
  U.S. consumption, 4
EPA, 136
ERDA, 114, 117

fan, circulation, 16
fiberglass panels, 23, 34

152

flat-basin collector, 38
flat-plate collector, 33, 34
flue, water, 68
forced convection, 18
fossil fuels, 3–6, 11, 113
furnace, solar, 53, 56

garbage recycling, 135
generator, 78, 95
  wind, 97, 105
geothermal energy, 82
glazing, solar, 22, 25
Granpa's Knob (wind plant), 107
greenhouse, passive-system, 22
greenhouse effect, 14, 22, 38, 57
grinding stones, 66

hard tech, 18, 33
head (water), 68
heat
  exchanger, 38
  flow, 18
  storage, 19, 29, 32, 41, 44
  trap, 18
high-absorbancy paint, 29, 36
high-tech systems, 8, 33
home, solar, 21
hydraulic marble machine, 64
hydroelectric power, 4, 63

impulse turbine, 78
indirect system (solar), 31
instant solar collector, 14
insulation, 21, 24, 29, 36, 61
integrated systems, 139–45
inverter (DC to AC), 78, 97

KWH (kilowatt hours), 103
kinetic energy, 66, 87

liquid junction cell, 59
liquid system collector, 36
longwave light, 14
low-tech systems, 8

manometer, 133
manure (methane), 130
methane
  gas, 130
  digester, 130–34
  manure, 130
  slurry, 131–133
M.I.T. solar house, 12

natural gas, 4–5
New Alchemy Inst., 140
newspaper logs, 120
non-renewable fuels, 5
nuclear
  accidents, 115
  agencies, 113
  energy, 3–4, 113–117
  expense, 115
  fusion, 117
  plants in U.S., 115
  potential, 117
  wastes, 114, 116

ocean power, 81
oil embargo, 3
orienting to sun, 19
overshot water wheel, 66

parabolic collector, 49
paraffin (heat storage), 32
passive systems, 19, 21
passive-system greenhouse, 22
Pelton water wheel, 78–79
penstock, 64, 67
photovoltaic
  battery charger, 47
  cell, 45, 47
  effect, 45, 47, 58
plastic film, 22, 29
plutonium, 117
Poncelot water wheel, 67
potential (water power), 68

radiation
  nuclear, 115
  thermal, 18
radioactive wastes, 114–116
reaction turbine, 78
reflecting surface, 24, 49
rock bed, 32
rock tumbler wheel, 70–76

safety, nuclear, 115–116
sailing ship, 87, 110
sails, windmill, 88
Savonius wind rotor, 104–106
sawdust stove, 128
Sea Horse, 81
slip ring assembly, 97
sluice, water, 68
slurry, methane, 131–133
soft tech, 19

solar
  availability, 12
  collector, instant, 14
  collector orientation, 20
  cooker, 49
  doghouse, 59
  energy, 11–61
  furnace, 4, 55
  future, 57
  glazing, 22
  history, 12
  home, 21
  in space, 59
  still, 12, 57
  water heater, 12, 36, 38
solstice
  summer, 20
  winter, 20
spirit level, 90
steam engine, 48
storage, heat, 19, 29, 32
stove
  sawdust, 128
  wood, 125-127
subsistence farm, 140
Sun-lite, 23, 34
supernatant (methane), 131
synergistic relationship, 139

Teflon film, 22
thermal
  energy, 14, 16
  mass, 22
  radiation, 14
thermosiphoning
  effect, 18, 25
  heater, 39
Thomason, Harry, 12
torque, windmill, 88, 97

turbine
  water, 78
  wind, 107

Union of Concerned Scientists, 115
ultraviolet rays, 34
uranium, 113

vanes, wind, 88
velocity, wind, 89
vertical water wheel, 66
voltage regulator, 95

waterbed, 31
water distillation, 12, 55
water drums, 29
water heater
  solar, 36, 38
  thermosiphoning, 39
water power, 63–85
  availability, 63
  future, 84
  history, 64
  ocean, 81
water wheel, 64, 66, 70
wave power, 81
wind gauge, 90
windmill, 88, 92, 94
  annular, 94
  bicycle wheel, 98
  water-pumping, 94
wind power, 87–110
  availability, 88
  electricity generated, 95
  future, 107
  generator, 97
  history, 92
wind velocity, 88
wood stove, 125–127
wood waste, 125